How to Activate The Hidden Power of God in You

How to use Meditation, Visualization, Affirmation, and Self-Hypnosis for Optimal Success

Mac Drinker

How to Activate the Hidden Power of The God in You: How to Use Meditations, Visualizations, Affirmations, and Self-Hypnosis for Optimal Success

Mac Drinker

Published by: 10-10-10 Publishing Markham, Ontario

Contents

DEDICATION

This work is dedicated to the many people who strive daily to make a better life for themselves and others. I hope this work will bring valuable information to help you reach your goals. A special dedication to my mother, Channie Langston-Taylor. Rest in love, Mom. You have given me an excellent example of what respect, love, kindness, and integrity mean. Words cannot express my admiration and love for you. Finally, to my wife, Donna R. Lewis-Drinker, thank you for your love, support, and encouragement. You have been by my side and always reminded me that all is possible.

FOREWORD

I am pleased to recommend *How to Activate the Hidden Power of God In You,* by Mac Drinker. The tools in this book are easy and practical. You can use them to awaken the God within you and reach your goals quickly. You can use deep breathing techniques to relax and meditate. Use affirmations to confirm your desire is authentic and in action. Learn how to recognize your dream and make it your vision board. You will be able to quickly reach the alpha state of mind and be capable of accessing various transformative practices such as meditation, visualizations, affirmation, and hypnosis. Embrace the profound journey to explore and unlock the highest potential within and activate the hidden power of God in you.

Use the meditation technique in this work to explore and cultivate deep peace, inner wisdom, and a profound sense of unity with the divine. You activate the hidden power in this sacred space, aligning yourself with the religious and spiritual course. Learn how to align your chakras, experience empowerment, and create vivid mental images of your divine desires. It is never too late to engage your imagination and tap into the limitless potential of your mind. The visualization and hypnosis portion of this book will give you a double dose of attuning to communicate with the universe.

Affirmation, the power of spoken words, acts as a bridge between your conscious and subconscious mind. By choosing empowering words and repeating them with conviction, you imprint positive beliefs and attention into your subconscious, aligning yourself with the divine truth. Affirmations enable you to transcend self-limiting thoughts and replace them with the divine affirmations of abundance, love, and joy. Through this practice, you open yourself to receiving the blessings and miracles God has in store for you.

Hypnosis is a powerful state that helps you recognize and focus on hidden suggestibility that offers a gateway to the subconscious mind. By entering a state of deep relaxation, you become receptive to positive suggestions and healing transformations. Under the guidance of a skilled practitioner or through self-hypnosis techniques, you can assess the subconscious realm and reprogram limited beliefs, aligning yourself with the divine blueprint that resides within you.

Within these pages, you will discover a rich blueprint of practical techniques that can be easily replicated. You will learn different insights that combine the force of meditation, visualization, affirmation, and hypnosis. Through their integration, you will embark on a holistic journey of self-discovery and spiritual transformation. You will learn to navigate the depths of meditation, harvest the creative power of visualization, craft affirmation, and infuse them in divine truth. When you explore the potential depth of hypnosis, you will assess your inner third rim for ultimate success. Embark on this sacred path, embrace it with an open mind and heart, trust in divine guidance, and gain a profound reverence. Activating the hidden power of God within is a heavenly collaboration where your intention aligns with the highest good for yourself and all people.

Raymond Aaron

New York Times Bestselling Author

ACKNOWLEDGMENTS

I give praise to the most merciful, the most graceful, the most honorable, the most loving God. I believe that grace is consistent with facts and reality, and truth is not something you believe; the truth is something you know. You shall know the truth, and the truth shall set you free; John 8:32 KJV. I want to thank my wife and children for their patience, understanding, and support. My lovely mother (rest in love and peace, Mom) for teaching me how to be a god-fearing person, Donna Lewis-Drinker, my better half; your support, patience, and admiration made me a better husband. You never gave up on me; you put up with me during the tough times of our marriage. I am grateful to you. I will always love and cherish you until the end of my life.

Thanks to Brenda Doughtery, clinical nurse (VAMC Jesse Brown Hospital, Chicago), for supporting me like a mother and standing up for me when I could not stand for myself. You made me see the good in myself and helped make me a better person. Thank you for fighting for me. I am incredibly grateful to Mr. Allen James Lynch, recipient of the Congressional Medal of Honor, for his conspicuous gallantry and intrepidity in action at the risk of his own life above and beyond the call of duty that earned him the highest honor in combat, the Congressional Medal of Honor. He never stopped fighting, even after the War. I will always be thankful for you advocating on my behalf and that of my family. You are a true hero.

I also want to acknowledge Mrs. Judy Copeland (Veteran Affairs Vocational Rehabilitation, Atlanta, GA.), an actual guidance counselor. This book never would have happened without your confidence and support. To Dr. Slayton and Mercer University, "Go Bearcats," you have inspired and motivated me to be the best I can be. You pushed me to never give up on circumstances and situations. I hope that this book will give some benefit to the reader. Thank you for being real because that is the only way to be.

CHAPTER 1: TURNING YOUR FAITH INTO REALITY

A Perspective

God created humans in his image, and in the image of God created them; male and female created them. KJV Chapter 1: 27

To activate the hidden power of the god person, they must first realize that they are living gods. To start the god within the inner self, or the subconscious self. Another intended purpose of activating the hidden powers is to take hold of the tools and concepts in this book, strengthen the inner mind, heal the body, and create one's reality. Indeed, great concepts and scriptures in the Bible will undoubtedly help. It is a controversial subject used to gain prosperity; we must understand the deep spiritual values of the biblical scriptures. According to the scriptures, humans are made in the image of God. If we believe this to be true, we believe there is someone, something, or an entity more powerful, knowledgeable, and foresought than male or female. Our responsibility is to find that truth and become powerful and more potent because of our beliefs. You must believe in your inner person to make your dream a reality. God is a creator; you are a creator as well. Yeshua (Jesus) said, "What I can do, you can also do even greater things" (John 14: 12), and he raised the dead, healed the sick, and fished gold out of the sea.

Therefore, knowing who you are and accepting the inner you will give you greater confidence in your ability to create. Although there are many viewpoints and different thoughts from people on the religious side of the argument, most humans have some belief system with similar significance to a creator source. The intent is for us to think like a godhead, see ourselves taking on the responsibility and inhibiting the god in persons and all things. To know thyself and know that creation is within humans and is human is divine. Furthermore, the thoughts of humans are an existential part of creation. It has its existence from a spiritual perspective, and we can activate the god within to assist us in reaching our goals, our aspirations, and our desires.

When we take on the mindset that we can create because we are wonderfully made, we believe we can do more incredible things. When we take on the thought process, we are gods; we have already created in our god mind that we are powerful, and what our mind can conceive will be achieved. Keep in mind that we believe this to be true. Therefore, we are (to be), li (to lie in a particular state), and eve (to eve, forever growth). Remember, to believe, we must first recognize that the lie must exist, and for a lie to live, there must be some truth. The truth is that which is consistent with facts and reality. The truth is not something you believe; the truth is something you know. Therefore, I want to give you as much truth as possible. "You shall know the truth, and the truth shall set you free." The truth is, you are created in the image of God, made in triple darkness that, over time, eventually became a light being. You are a living part of the divine spirit—all things in the universe are the creator's consciousness. Therefore, when one asks the holy spirit in sincerity and truth, their desired result must manifest that which is chosen by thought, speech, and light. Finally, the trees, the grass, and all animate and inanimate things are of God made in his lightness.

Your thoughts are the creative spark that assists in the belief that "I Am" and I will; instead of using the God concept, you can use whatever means necessary to obtain the same result. For instance, one can use source energy, creator, or higher power as synonymous with their God. But know that you are made of the Godhead's spirit, consciousness, and physical being. On the spiritual level, one is consistently dealing with positive attributes of self, negative attributes of self, and neutral attributes of nature, and becoming aware of the constantly ongoing battle of self and God. We as human beings constantly search for the inner self, the God inside (the unconsciousness, the unknown), to bring what we desire into reality.

Dreams and visions, which we will discuss later in the text, seem real from the inside, but a dream or vision is only an abstract version of who one is or wants to be. Therefore, we are always living in the past, present, and future self; I am the God within.

Having Dominion over Your Life

"Let us make human in our image, after our likeness, and let them have dominion over the fish of the sea, the fowls of the air, the cattle, and the earth."

Genesis 1:26

When you wake up during the grand raising (morning) and must be at work at nine o'clock AM, but instead of getting out of bed an hour earlier, you decide to hit the snooze at eight fifty-five AM, you have lost a significant part of your dominion. You have lost control. On the other hand, when you set the clock at 7:45 AM and sleep until eight o'clock AM, you give yourself a certain amount of control without stress. You now have dominion over your body and mind; you are back in time. When you have direct control of your inner or subconscious, as well as your body, you have dominion. The god in humans. What exactly does having dominion mean? According to the website vocabulary.com, dominion means that you oversee or rule something; you have dominion over it. If your mind tells you it is time to get started, but your body tells you to sleep a little longer, ask yourself, "Is that dominion over the body or mind?

Because we are humans and made in the image of the creators, we were given certain qualities to give us dominion over animate and inanimate objects and fowls of the air. One of the qualities we have is free will. The ability to have free will and the ability to make rational decisions give us a distinct advantage over other mammals. Not only do free will and conscious thought give us dominion over the earth, but they also give us the authority to command and the freedom to create. In essence, this gives us great power to subdue and sustain that which is good. Ask yourself the question: Do you have authority over your body and mind? Wouldn't it be great if you did have this control? Continue to read this book until the end and prove to me it can be done. When you have authority over your body and mind, you have activated the gift of authority. The gift of authority was given to us when we activated the god person's consciousness and could control it. The story of the great fall of man as an interpreter in the Bible did not prevent humans from God's power. Man or woman may fail, but God never fails; even the god in you never fails. You could command and receive the authority you possess inside, practicing the tools and techniques in the book, and reign supreme over your life by being aware that you could command your body and mind to attract that which you desire—authority over life.

Finally, what happens when one fails to recognize the psychology of not being in control of one's body and mind? A lack of dominion or lack of control in the psychological world is called irrational thoughts or abnormal thoughts. This may, in terms, lead to cognitive distortion. Two main enemies of the mind may cause either irrational thoughts or cognitive distortion, which are incidents from the past or the unconscious taking control. This past event, or future anticipation of some events, lacks the capability to think straight; it could be trauma, fear, or apprehension. In fact, this trauma, fear, or apprehension is causing a constant interpretation of your reality in an unhealthy way. For example, what if you argued with someone in your family, disengaged from the argument, and walked away? Later, you hear the family member talking to another family member in another room. You would immediately think the family member is talking about your earlier argument. This false sense of reality may lead to unrealistic beliefs that can be hard to overcome and can create unhealthy habits. You lose somewhat of the advantage of your dominion over yourself. You can re-align yourself by meditating, visualizing, affirming, and using hypnosis to overcome any distorted reality. Rekindle the essence of the inner-God by activating the god in you. Gain that dominion — the Electro-magnetic You.

"Thank you for making me so wonderfully complex! Your workmanship is marvelous—how well I know."

Psalm 139:14 New Living Translation

Have you ever wondered why we are one of the few species that walk upright and can walk for a long period of time? Scientists believe that humans once walked on all four limbs and could walk upright because they needed to secure food from trees. Humans would pick the food from the trees and return it to their dwelling. As a result, their bodies developed into an upright position over time. But another reason is that the body provides more energy in the upright position. The human body is constructed like an antenna, constantly absorbing naturally occurring magnetic waves from the universe. These waves postulate or act as a massager to raise or lower the flow of vibrations. These vibrations affect the nervous system and other body parts and can affect humans' emotions, characteristics, intelligence, and nature. The nervous system generates the flow of electromagnetic current to the pineal gland, throughout the spinal cord, and to the root chakra to regulate the body's metabolism, which assists in grounding.

The fact that we are composed of electromagnetic fields is proof that informs us that there is an invisible force of energy within us and our environment. This energy can be moved forward or backward from each state of the body. Consider this example: an erected wire of the correct length on your rooftop can detect electromagnetic waves and pick out pulses related to its own length. The waves are turned into a variety of electric currents. The converted electromagnetic waves reach the electronic equipment in your home and translate it into television pictures. Your body has a natural antenna made in the image of God, which will detect the electromagnetic waves from your thoughts, specifically made to receive radiant energy from the universe.

The vibrations result from the electromagnetic waves on the body and can have positive or negative consequences on a person's behavior and character. These vibrations exist in people, animals, inanimate objects, and that which has not materialized into reality. The human body is comprised of electromagnetic fields that can interact with the physical body and its functions. These energy fields include light and color, sound, thermal energies, and heat. These energy fields may be activated by using some of the techniques in the book. The main purpose of the chapter is to give some basic understanding of how electromagnetic waves from the environment may affect us when we manifest our reality. By bringing the body under subjection and controlling the frequency of the electromagnetic fields to the body, we can more easily activate the subconscious within us to do our bidding.

Whether you want great health, healing power, prosperity, or joy, you must first raise your vibration. To control negative thoughts, suspicious behaviors, and suggestive statements, raise your electromagnetic vibration to its highest level. You will speak into reality that which you say is so. The negative thoughts and vibrations accumulated from the electromagnetic waves can result from some trauma or an event that does not align with your body frequencies. When you reach a higher vibration level, speak a powerful, positive gratitude statement to activate the god's power within. Affirmations are great for the morning sunrise. Say it with me, *"I am grateful for the creators and the source in me; I am grateful and pleased to be amongst the living; I am grateful to have great health and a sound mind; I am grateful to have a wonderful, amazing day every day, and I am grateful for the love, peace, and happiness you have given for me to enjoy this day, it is done."* You have just raised your vibration to a different level.

Everything Vibrates

To access the center of your God consciousness, to master your life purposes, to gain wisdom and insight, to accumulate more knowledge and retain it, to gather more intellect, you must raise your body vibration to a level acceptable to your thought process. Now that we know that the body is an electromagnetic vessel, we can easily comprehend how our body vibrates. Think of it like this. When I was growing up, most children would have a spinning top in their toy box. The human body is similar. If you hit it hard enough, it will react; just like the harder you spin a top, the faster it goes. Not only would the top spin, but it would also make a woofing noise while it was spinning fast. When it slowed down, the sound would leave, and the top would start to wobble before it stopped. Your body is vibrating like a spinning top at high speed, but sometimes, when you are out of mental alignment, you slow down like the spinning top and want to stop. On the one hand, when your vibrations are at a higher level, you are happier and more peaceful, you gain more spiritual support from others, and you have access to more wisdom, insight, and guidance. Spiritual healing is available. On the other hand, when your vibrations slow down, the complete opposite may happen.

How do we raise our vibration to a higher level to support our spiritual, mental, and physical health? First, we want to ensure our body is aligned with the electromagnetic current in the body. The body acts as a superconductor, regulating the flow of the electromagnetic current without resistance, with the loss of pure energy. Remember, this energy is affected by light, color, sound, and harmony. Scientists believe that each cell in the body is an energy field with consciousness. Each body organ relates to cells with their own characteristics and vibrations that control their function. The transmitting bioelectromagnetic field controls the emotion. This vibrating energy field directly affects a person's physical, mental, emotional, and spiritual state. By maintaining an open and smooth energy field, we can prevent the onset of emotional, mental, physical, and spiritual breakdown.

When we align our chakras with divine reality, we can raise our vibrations to a higher level of consciousness. In this book, I have dedicated several sections to the type of chakra alignment I have used over the years, with great success in treating severe combat post-traumatic stress disorder. The goal is to raise the vibration to a higher spiritual level. Think about the spinning top I mentioned earlier. When the string is released at the beginning of the spin, the vibrations of the top flow smoothly, straight, and in complete balance. The use of prayer and supplication from a spiritual aspect of raising vibrations is the most powerful for anxiety. I use prayer for positive affirmations to raise my vibrations. You may also recognize both positive and negative attributes that may appear in your life, and the bridge between a person and their god. To become aware of the god in self is to be aware of the highest aspect of self. To obtain your highest senses, activate and align the body's bioelectric-magnetic electrons, protons, and neutrons of the body system by raising your vibrations.

The Importance of Prayer to Your Source Energy

This is the age of great fear: fear of viruses, fear of plagues, fear of war, fear of political unrest. Every day, the news media inundates us with more news of fears: fears of crime, fears of the price of food, fears of gun violence, fear, fear, and more fear. What do we do? What is our recourse? How do we continue to move toward being a God-like person? How do we calm the savage beast within us? In some way or another, we pray. Whether we recognize that we are praying or simply asking for some spiritual help, we are still praying; according to Merriam-Webster online definition, prayer is a petition to God in words or thoughts for help. Another definition of prayer is a solemn request or expression of thanks addressed to God or an object of worship. There is no right or wrong way to pray; some prostrate by sitting on their knees and facing the east, others pray in the sun's path, and others pray for hours. Some stand, others sit.

According to 1 Thessalonians 5:16-23, Christians are requested to pray without ceasing in a time of distress and chaos. Praying without ceasing simply means always having our minds on the goodness of the creator God. The purpose of prayer is to strengthen the inner self when the soul is vexed or has a problem. Prayer brings out our humble, God-like character for peace of mind. Prayer places us in a state of forgiveness and gratefulness, hoping that we will receive what we ask for. Because prayer is a thought, we must be mindful of our thoughts when thinking of others. Make your thoughts your truth because you can never harm another person with your truths. Be mindful of what you think or say, because once thought of or said, you can never take it back. Yeshua (Jesus) taught that humans do not know how to pray or what to pray for. Therefore, we must be careful because of the power of the tongue; one's thoughts, when said or thought of in malice or anger, can harm a person.

Religion forms a community with the same beliefs in agreement, embedded by the same values or rules of the majority. There are also communal prayers amongst certain religious groups; when members share the same belief and agree, the members are embedded in those agreements or rules when praying. In addition, communal prayer is supposed to be the most powerful prayer for Christians. Communal prayer is done with supplication for another member. When one uses the practice of prayer, the divine attributes of character bring peace, happiness, and joy with divine thoughts.

Finally, from my personal experience, prayer helped me in the past, and I am weeping about the benefit today. We must learn how to pray without ceasing and pray the right way. There is a method of prayer for me. I was meditating during my salutation in the early morning hours between 2 and 4 o'clock AM. During this time, our electromagnetic waves are not corrupted by noise from cars and other mechanicals. Free spirits are awakened during this time after midnight to help you with your thoughts and aspirations. The most important thing at this point is to recognize that doubt is illuminated, and you can feel the inner self connecting with God within and without. Don't doubt what you asked for, but believe at that moment that it has already been received. Believe that the creator has already given you what you desire and ask for. Focus on the positive attributes, forgiving, and asking for forgiveness. Send out good thoughts for others, and vow to love others as you love yourself.

CHAPTER 2:
THE CORRECT WAY TO BREATHE

The Importance of Breathing Through the Nostrils

Do you want to transform your life into an unstoppable wealth magnet? Do you want to have great health? Do you want to travel with your family and friends without worries about finances and live stress-free? I believe this chapter is the cornerstone and foundation to help you get into your meditation faster and create your dream life. This chapter is about breathing the correct way to help your body relax. We gain spiritual, mental, and physical benefits when we breathe correctly, and we get the benefits of releasing stress and anxiety from the body. Therefore, we want to breathe correctly and obtain the maximum amount of oxygen needed to fill the lungs and distribute the oxygen to the cells faster. After reading this chapter and performing the exercise given, your lungs, respiratory system, and heart should be stronger. Furthermore, you should be able to relax your body quickly and get into your alpha state more rapidly. We start correcting our breathing by understanding a little bit about the nostrils and how they function.

Scientists have studied the anatomy of the human nostril for centuries, and continue to find different functions it performs. There are small vessels that lead from the sphenoidal sinus to the brain, and scientists have yet to discover their functions. Therefore, we will focus only on the area that gives us a basic understanding of how we should breathe. The nostril is the only proper way to inhale air into the body and exhale air out of the body. The nostril has two narrow channels or passageways in the middle of the face. These passageways contain strains of brisk hair, which serve to clean air from impurities when inhaling, warming the air before it travels to the olfactory receptor for delivery to the lungs. These strains of hair also filter bad air when it is expelled during exhalation, trapping excess oxygen and returning this oxygen back to the body. The olfactory receptors, consisting of the olfactory and supporting cells, are at the top of the nasal cavity; spongy-like tissue that further warms the air to body temperature to be provided to the lungs. Remember that the air moves through the nasal passage into the lungs when inhaled.

We are mostly focused on how the air moves through the nasal and thoracic cavities directly into the lungs and heart. When the intercostal muscles within the abdominal cavity move, they expand the lungs and create a passage for air to move into the navel, thoracic cavity, and lungs. When the intercostal muscle retracts, the lungs contract and the air is expelled from the lungs. Most organs, tissues, and glands comprise that portion of the trunk between the neck and the abdomen. Because of the quick movement of the chest when breathing, scientists once thought breathing from the chest was the proper way to breathe. However, we now know that using all the respiratory muscles is the proper and correct way to breathe.

High Chest Breathing

Breathing naturally and properly can give you more vitality, power, and energy while also activating the body's sympathetic nervous system. The sympathetic nervous system is responsible for many functions; one of the primary functions is to work in conjunction with the autonomic nervous system, which prepares your body for stress-related activities, fight or flight incidents, or sports activities. The sympathetic nervous system is responsible for increasing heart rate and can cause high blood pressure if not regulated properly. Remember that air is breathed through the nostrils, passing through the olfactory receptors; the olfactory receptor filters and prevents any unwanted elements from passing into the nasal cavity. After leaving the nasal cavity, air passes through the pleural cavity of the thorax, pushed into the lungs, heart, blood vessels, and other parts of the body through the chest. Therefore, we can assume that chest breathing is healthful in regulating and providing air quickly into the heart.

However, there are three distinct breathing techniques: chest, mid, and abdomen. We will discuss chest breathing here and its effect on the breathing system. Chest breathing or collarbone breathing was, at one time, the only breathing technique taught as the proper way to breathe. For many years, people were told to breathe through the chest; in other words, when the chest expands and retracts, it is called one breath. This type of breathing was great for activating the sympathetic nervous system and preparing athletes to run a marathon. Although high chest breathing techniques are great for athletes, they do not provide enough air for optimal health. Furthermore, it is not a technique you would want to use for meditating because it raises the heart rate too high to relax.

The high chest breathing technique elevates the rib cage while raising the collarbone; breathing from the chest also pushes the air against the diaphragm, allowing it to move up into its proper position. Incidentally, when air is pushed into the chest, the diaphragm quickly pushes forward while the shoulder moves slightly backward and down. Although the high chest breathing technique expands the chest, the air is forced into the lungs too quickly. As a result, the lungs cannot receive the proper amount of air to their full capacity. The lungs, air passage, the pleural chamber of the thorax, the median line, the heart, blood vessels, and the air tube are used to create breathing.

High chest breathing is used for rapid breathing to stimulate the sympathetic nervous system. It encourages the fight or flight mood and is most often used by athletes, such as boxers or MMA fighters. Use this breath sparingly when focusing on the exhale only, push the air out quickly, and make small, sharp, short breaths like a sneeze. Avoid moving your face or shoulder; let them relax naturally and allow the abdomen to drop. Again, when practicing the high chest breathing technique, inhale through the nostrils, hold for a few seconds, and exhale through the nostrils. Never inhale from the mouth or exhale from the mouth; this type of breathing is unhealthy.

Mid-level breathing or (diaphragm breathing)

The mid-level breathing level, mid-breathing, or rib breathing consists of breathing from the rib cage using the obliquus externus muscles. When you are breathing from the mid-level position, the diaphragm is pushed outward, the mid-section of the body expands, and the chest rises, filling the lungs with air. Although the chest is expanded, the air is released too fast for the chest to expand fully. As a result, the lungs are partially open, and not enough air is released into the lungs; one reason is that the air is pushed through the thorax spontaneously. Like chest breathing, the diaphragm is pushed outward instead of upward; therefore, the lungs cannot fully expand and receive the greatest amount of air.

The diaphragm is one of the most important parts of the body, and it helps you inhale and exhale. It is a muscle that sits below the lungs and heart. The diaphragm is a muscle attached to your sternum (a bone in the middle of your chest), the bottom of the rib cage, and your spine. The air is drawn into the lungs by raising the diaphragm, which acts as a semi-voluntary muscle that expands the side of the chest and lungs. That is why the diaphragm is pushed outward instead of upward when breathing from the midribs. Consequently, this type of breathing allows the diaphragm to push upwards, the abdomen to draw in, the ribs to rise, and the chest to partially expand. This may be a quick way to breathe in air, but it will not completely fill the lungs. Mid-breathing is most useful for swimmers who must quickly pull air into the lungs, hold the air, and then expel it through the nose.

Again, because the diaphragm moves outward, as in the high-breathing technique, not enough air flows into or is retained by the lungs, high breathing moves the chest upward, and the shoulder moves upward and backward, whereas mid-breathing raises the chest forward, keeping the arms steady and not moving the shoulder slightly backward. There is nothing wrong with breathing from the chest or rib. However, you are not obtaining the maximum amount of air needed to fulfill your purpose of activating the parasympathetic nervous system, respiratory system, and cardiovascular system.

Combining high and mid-breathing may provide the right air for swimmers, astronauts, pilots, etc. But these techniques do not fare well with joggers, runners, or singers. You can also expect to do well using these techniques to lower heart rates and blood pressure and stimulate the parasympathetic nervous system for rest. Although the breathing technique does not provide the maximum amount of air to the respiratory system, it does provide enough air to the lungs to purify the blood.

Fresh air helps the blood carry nutrients to every body part to activate hormones and other chemicals. You will be able to send this energy to different organs in the body and increase life forces for healing and ultimate health. When you breathe correctly, the different fluids, hormones, chromones, etc., properly support the organs and cells of the body. Therefore, it is vitally important that everyone knows the proper way to breathe when healing, meditating, or just relaxing. Now, you know a little about the two methods of breathing we have been using throughout our lives.

Abdominal Breathing (deep breathing)

The third and most important breathing technique is abdominal breathing, which is called deep breathing. Buddhist monks have practiced the deep breathing technique for thousands of years in most Asian countries of the East. The Western hemisphere has only recently started using deep breathing techniques in meditation and relaxation therapies. This technique is used in group therapy and other therapeutic settings. It is a relativity simple technique but takes practice to perfect for long-term effect. Abdominal breathing has several physical benefits as well, such as promoting a healthy posture, promoting a healthy diaphragm, and relieving stress and tension in the body.

Abdominal breathing is what I call spirit breathing, the first motion to obtain complete breathing. Deep breathing is used for meditation, visualization, hypnosis, prayers, mantras, and healing. I can go on and on. Deep breathing has become more prominent in childcare institutions, elementary schools, and high schools to help students deal with stress and everyday life. Extended practice of deep breathing exercises will promote a powerful sense of awareness. Incidentally, because abdominal breathing starts at the lower part of the abdomen, it may enhance a sense of inner power, awakening the solar plexus, and promoting a sense of wellness.

The solar plexus is considered the center axis of the inner body, and unifies the inner body with nature. The solar plexus is also considered the sun source of the human body systems, and as a result, it is where we receive our life force energy source, the god within. The deep breathing technique provides an avenue for the complete breathing system. Deep breathing techniques, when performed, allow the other two techniques, mid-breathing and high chest breathing, to function correctly. When you only breathe from the chest, it is not the correct breathing form to properly expand the diaphragm and abdominal muscles.

The stomach muscle must first be activated for abdominal breathing in order to practice deep breathing. When the stomach is activated, it is considered stable; when the stomach is stable, slowly and gently push the lower stomach outward. When the stomach is pushed outward, imagine the diaphragm pushing upward; this is the muscle between your stomach and lower rib. The diaphragm pushes upward instead of outward, the lower ribs expand, the lungs expand, expanding the chest, and the shoulder goes upper and down. Hence, when air is pulled into the nostril, it passes through the nasal cavity or nasal passage into the chest cavities, the lungs, the heart and its vessels, the blood cells, and different body parts because of the abdominal muscle. Abdominal breathing assists in expanding the lower, mid, and chest areas to allow the maximum amount of air into the respiratory system. The stomach moves out and into the solar plexus, the diaphragm moves upward into the heart chakras, and the chest is fully expanded. You are now taking in the maximum amount of air needed to activate and energize certain body parts.

We want to always use the deep breathing technique for meditations, visualizations, affirmations, and hypnosis practices. This type of breathing is called the union breathing system or complete breathing system, where we unify the three methods of breathing as one. Although the complete breathing method, when used correctly, benefits the spiritual, inner-God-life self, it also benefits the physical, correct body posture, builds self-confidence, and improves overall health. The best and simplest way to perfect the complete breathing system is to practice the 4x4x4 method used in the next section.

The Complete Deep Breathing System

ribs, or diaphragm breathing; and high chest breathing, with practice, become union breathing, or the complete deep breathing technique. To practice the complete deep breathing system, we will use the 4x4x4 method. We always want to breathe in through the nostrils and breathe out through the nostrils, considering all the different movements of the different techniques. The stomach or abs move outward, the diaphragm moves upward, and the chest and shoulder expand and move upward and back. First, try to perfect one method at a time, noticing each position of the inner section of the body.

Again, we want to use the 4x4x4 method to allow the air to fill the lungs completely and be distributed to the heart and its vessels. Let's try this method one time so we can get a better understanding of how it is used: inhale slowly through your nostrils while noticing: one, the stomach moving outward; two, the diaphragm moving upward; three, the chest expanding; and four, the shoulders moving upward and back. During this count of four, you will fill the air entering the nostrils and filling the lungs, then hold the breath for a count of four, and finally, relax the body completely for a count of four. When exhaling, notice the lower abs moving back inward, the diaphragm moving downward, the chest deflating, and the shoulder dropping back down, relaxing the body. Being mindful to always breathe through the nostrils is very important.

Complete breathing techniques provide the proper amount of air for the organs and cells of the body. This keeps the diaphragm in perfect alignment and functioning properly. It allows the ribs or thorax cavity to have normal breathing and allows enough air in the lungs for distribution. The complete breathing cycle includes all the benefits of the high chest and mid-breathing techniques. The complete breathing system brings into play the entire respiratory system and activates and ascends the body into the esoteric inner phase of being and the exoteric outer phase of the human being.

The science of the body is connected to the complete breathing system, whereas the body is unique to God, the creator. We can activate the God-within by practicing the complete breathing system. The technique can be practiced while sitting, standing, or kneeling. After several weeks of practicing each technique, begin to practice breathing as one continuous motion. Continue to practice the complete breathing technique until it becomes normal to you as one breath. Use the 4x4x4 method, close your eyes, become aware of any tension, relax those tense areas, feel the breath filling the lungs, become aware of your breathing, and practice until the three techniques become one normal way of breathing. When practicing and with time, you will become aware that you are breathing the correct way: inhaling through your nostrils with the mouth closed and exhaling carbon dioxide through the nostrils with the mouth closed, trapping any excess oxygen and returning it back into the body. Try these secret breathing techniques while positioning or prostrating on your knees. Try the techniques while lying down, with your legs raised, and try to touch your feet. You will be quite surprised, as you continue to use these methods, by the quality of life you can obtain and the control you will eventually gain over your mind, body, and health. As we move closer to understanding the body's mechanics, we will understand the significance of this type of breathing and how it affects how we meditate and manifest.

CHAPTER 3:
YOUR BODY IS A HUMAN ANTENNA

We Are Made Up of Electromagnetic currents

Some who study the Sumerian Tables say, "The world has its misconception about what angels really look like. Elohim (angels) are simple electromagnetic currents, supposedly from other dimensions or galaxies, who come as a spiritual being, to guide in spiritual form." In this case, we will assume that the body is an electromagnetic entity with its own frequencies, vibrations, and pulsation; it is pure energy vibrating within the universe and carries its own currents. Therefore, you, the human, may act as an angel. But how do we control these currents? How do we communicate with the angels? We have stated that the body is an electromagnetic current.

There are three types of currents. First, the free flow of electrons flows through metal or copper wiring, which are currents carrying electricity from one area to another. Because this current consists of metal objects, the body does not have this type; it can only flow through metal wires and is used for communication from one point to another, i.e., electricity. Secondly, there are electric currents such as ionic currents, which are most often found in batteries, and power our electric cars and lawn mowers. Ions are atoms or molecules within water that create their own surplus of electrons. This type of current is very large and stays charged for long periods of time. Incidental ion currents are found in the body but do not impact its systems. Finally, the third current type is semiconduction, which can act as a natural semiconductor in the body. Incidentally, since the discovery of semiconductors in 1930, through further research, scientists have created a small electric current that was capable of passing through the crystals. It has created a mega revolution in quantum theory and has become the basis of the high-tech revolution. The science of semiconductors has also made the evolution of AI (artificial intelligence) possible. However, the natural intelligence of the human body also depends on semiconduction.

So, how does this relate to the human antenna discussed in the book? According to Wikipedia, an antenna contains an array of conductors electrically connected to the receiver or transmitter. Antennas are designed to transmit and receive radio waves. Our bodies are also semiconductors able to transmit and receive what we desire from the universe. Because we are made up of electromagnetic waves, we can also receive and transmit messages that are unseen from dimension to dimension, transmitting and receiving information from source intelligence. The antenna for transmitting and receiving radio waves comprises different RF current-carrying components, such as passive metal receiving elements and a preamplifier to capture microwave frequencies. These components are designed to couple their connections to the electromagnetic field, or radio waves, which carry signals through the air or space at the speed of light. Because there is evidence that super-conduction exists in living matter and electromagnetic currents are vibrating in humans, it may be possible to communicate, transmit, and receive messages from the universe.

Humans are a harmonic system, and subsystems with energy fields interacting with one another. Each cell is an energy system within itself, connecting with consciousness, creating vibrations, and making up the electric component membranes that create the electromagnetic fields of the body system. Each organ comprises cells that create the same harmonic signal to function. In addition, each organ has its own characteristics, vibrating and waiting for commands to receive, monitor, and control its functions. Each person has their own unique energy field surrounding them and waits for activation from the pineal glands throughout the spinal cord. The seven chakras are uniquely positioned to electrify and activate the electromagnetic currents along their cord.

Spinal Cord is a Magnetic Source

When we acknowledge that we are electromagnetic currents, electromagnetic waves vibrating within the universe, we better understand how our body system creates its frequencies. We are the gods of the earth, source energy, light energy, able to activate the God within. With practice, we can vibrate outside of the physical sphere, moving within the rim of different dimensions. According to physics, your location at a particular time creates your position; we call this the fixed reference point of our origin. We can control this reference point by aligning ourselves with that which we desire. Our most important responsibility is to subdue and protect the time and space we are placed in when we are born. Subdue means to control the earth and everything in it. I ask, are we in control of everything in our space? Are we in control of our bodies? If not, why not? We are the gods of this earth. What happened? What went wrong?

May I say nothing happened? We are still in control, and we create our own world and the space we live in at the appointed time. We were meant to be, to create, to control, to have, and to subdue that which was appointed by the god within. However, we lost some very important knowledge that once made us the gods that we were created to be, and that knowledge was the knowledge of self.

Humans can activate the god within by knowing about ourselves and how to activate some very important attributes. And the Lord God commanded the humans, saying,

"Of every tree of the garden, thou mayest freely eat; But of the tree of the knowledge of good and evil, thou shalt not eat of it: for in the day that thou eat thereof, thou shalt surely die."

(Genesis 2: 16-17)

Man was not given a certain time to die; he did not lose his God-given talent, but some of his abilities. The highest aspect of your being is not recognized at the beginning of birth. Before humans fell into the garden (Earth), we were endowed with our highest senses that were activated by the barathary gland, a gland that Westerners do not recognize.

The barathary gland is a gland that was initially inside the cavity of the hippocampus area of the brain, in the lower part of the cerebellum. The cerebellum is located at the lower part of the brain and is attached to the brain stem. The hippocampus is part of the limbic system and is involved with memory formation. The cerebellum lies posterior to the hindbrain and is attached to a stalk-like structure connecting the rest of the brain to the spinal cord. The cerebellum is responsible for movement and body control. The spinal cord is part of the midbrain, which is responsible for vision and links the forebrain to the hindbrain. Right before the spinal cord lies the medulla oblongata, which is responsible for controlling breathing, heartbeat, and blood supply.

This part of the brain is very important for life, and once played a significant function in the barathary gland. The barathary gland is where we receive our highest senses; telepathy is able to send messages and communicate from mind to mind; clairvoyance is the ability to see into other dimensions with a clear vision; psychometry is the ability to hold an individual and be able to tell everything about them; and intuition, the awareness of something before it happens. The spinal cord mediates between the brain, acting as an antenna to communicate with and connect the nervous system and other body systems. When we align the chakras of these systems, we can activate the god-like senses to accomplish a righteous task.

Understanding The Two Main Systems of the Body (Nervous, Endocrine)

The four higher senses or abilities we discussed in the last chapter were lost to some and obtained by others. When we align chakras, which we will discuss in the next chapter, over time, we will begin to fully understand and see ourselves as a light energy system, vibrating and rotating, creating light, color, sound, heat, thermal energy, magnetic, and electricity. These energy fields surround the human body to create the power that enables us to activate and raise our frequencies to a God-like level. Although we may never be like the creator, we are able to create our world in the space and time we live in by activating the body system.

According to scientists, eleven central systems keep our body functioning: t

- The endocrine system regulates the body's processes through hormone secretion and production.

- The nervous system, the primary center for sensory input and uses this input to elicit appropriate responses; the

- The respiratory system uses exchanged gases between the internal and external environment.

- The cardiovascular system, through blood circulation, transports gases, nutrients, and hormones that are turned into waste.

- The digestive system breaks down physical and chemical foods and allows for the absorption of nutrients.

- The lymphatic system maintains fluid balance and helps fight infections.

- The reproductive system reproduces cells to generate offspring.

- The urinary system filters blood and excretes waste from the body.

- The integumentary system protects against the external environment and regulates temperature.

- The skeletal system supports and protects internal organs.

- Muscular system, voluntary and involuntary movement.

Activating this system is the key to maintaining a healthy and productive lifestyle. When we activate the endocrine and nervous systems, we open the system for manifesting healing and optimal functioning.

Our bodies are antennas constricted to receive energy waves from the God source; the body may absorb naturally occurring electromagnetic waves, ready to send messages to another system of the body. The nervous system contains the framework for conducting the flow of electricity in the body. When we align the body properly, chemical hormones act as spiritual messages that emanate from the body through the bloodstream. The use of sounds and colors stimulates the endocrine and autonomic nervous systems and helps the body maintain optimum mental, physical, and spiritual health. Once the nervous and endocrine systems are activated, a pathway is opened to the energy field that creates the aura around the body.

The aura is a multicolored light around the body; this aura is our spiritual energy. Once the energy field vibrates, energy is channeled through the chakras, enhancing the higher senses, clairvoyance, telepathy, psychometry, and intuition. The spinal cord has seven major points within the physical body, called chakras, that act as a bridge between the nervous system and the endocrine system. Once these chakras are properly activated, they produce hormones that conduct and send messages to enhance the vibratory energy called the aura. The chakras and their points on the spinal cord activate the chemical codes in the endocrine system. Before we move into the chakras, let us encapsulate two important experiences of the body.

The Ability to Move Outside the Physical Sphere

Most out-of-body experiences (OBEs) have been difficult for scientists to understand, and the phenomenon has been studied for years with few results. The scientific phenomena have been difficult to explain and impossible to prove factual. Often associated with a sense of detachment, these experiences challenge our understanding of consciousness, perception, and the nature of reality. We will focus on exploring the concept of out-of-body experiences, their potential explanations in our lives, and their scientific and cultural significance.

Instead of calling it the phenomenon of out-of-body experiences, we will call it moving outside of the physical sphere. We are changing the narrative because our goal is to understand how mental experience through meditation might take us to the dimension of the outside of the physical rim, or quantum reality. Out-of-body experiences occur when an individual feels as if their consciousness has detached from their physical body and is able to observe their surroundings from a different vantage point. The phenomenon often involves, according to scientists, floating, flying, or hovering above one's own body. These experiences can occur from near-death experiences caused by an overdose of drugs, medications, sleep paralysis, or because of certain medical conditions. Moving outside of the physical is common in certain cultures and historical periods, adding a universal dimension to this intriguing phenomenon.

We will use meditation to move outside the physical sphere by visualizing, hypnosis, and activating the cerebellum when we understand that our out-of-body projection revolves around three distinct aspects: the neurological aspect, the altered states of consciousness aspect, and the multi-dimensional and quantum theories aspects of a person going out of the body sphere into different dimensions. First, let's observe the neurological perspective of the out-of-body projection phenomenon associated with the brain. We know that the part of the brain that normally affects the body is the cerebellum. If there is any chemical imbalance or lack of response, it is because of a lack of response from the parietal lobe. The cerebellum is part of the parietal lobe, responsible for integrating sensory information and spatial orientation, and it plays an important role in generating the sensation of detachment from the body.

The second thing we must know to move outside of the body's physical sphere is how altered states of consciousness affect our being. While we are in a meditation or sleep stage, we can move outside of the physical sphere. We can project ourselves out of the physical sphere and into new realities. Some researchers propose that these experiences arise from changes in brainwave patterns or neurotransmitter activity, which could alter one's perception of one's own body and surroundings. It is theorized that these altered states might enable individuals to access a different level of consciousness, allowing them to perceive their surroundings from an unconventional perspective.

The third and final aspect is the multi-dimensional and quantum theories. From a theoretical physics point of view, there is a link to the existence of parallel universes or higher dimensions, suggesting that it is possible through meditation and hypnosis to astral project an out-of-body experience. Quantum physics states that reality is not solely confined to observable universes and that consciousness might transcend our physical bodies to access different dimensions. Hence, we understand that to move outside the physical sphere, we must consider both the scientific and cultural significance, scientifically exploring the nature of consciousness, brain functioning, and the potential for other states of awareness, and utilizing our natural neuroimaging techniques and psychological mechanisms in our experiences. Finally, from a cultural perspective, we must encourage and enhance the arts, literature, and one's religious beliefs for the greater good to use out-of-body interpretation as evidence of the separation of the soul from the body when activating the god in self.

Light Energy

Before there was light, there was darkness, and the darkness is not light; we humans are made in the image of our god, and if God was light, then we are light. When we were once lost, we are now found because we are not blind. The light of God is the firmament of God, which one must see clearly. We are inundated with our auras shining brightly each day. These auras ignite energy throughout the universe, seeking that which is good. The light energy is magnetic and returns to the inner self as that which we visualize. When you do not have the right feeling about any situation, and it interferes with your aura, you move on. Your auras are affected by the vibration of the light in this space or time.

Light energy is the enlightenment of the soul by activating the nervous system through colored light. When you have the spirit of God, the soul of God, or the intelligence of God, you speak the light into existence. When light appears, and you are light energy, then darkness will disappear. Dispelling the darkness in one's life means raising one's light. When the darkness is divided from the light, the darkness and the sun will shine forever, dispelling the darkness and showing the pure matter of reality. God separated the light from the darkness (Genesis 1:4), and you are separated from the darkness as well. You can now create your new world within and shine your internal reality to that which is. Your auras will continue to expand their outer bloom for additional information and good.

The light energy within is controlled by the pineal gland, which is responsible for its ability to produce light and color. We are electromagnetic beings, and the vibration of our light energy cannot be seen or measured with the naked eye. This light vibration may create a thermal energy field of colors, reactivating the nine senses and supercharging one through time, space, and new dimensions. The pineal gland is part of the epithalamus of the brain that synthesizes melatonin. This light energy enhances the auras around our bodies, creating light and colors. With continuous actuation of the pineal gland through alignments, we activate the god in one internal consciousness.

Each person has a unique energy field that captures light energy and dispenses it back into the universe. This light energy is accessed from a universal pool known as the universal life force. This energy in the life force comes into the body through each chakra, and its transforming qualities dominate the senses and emotional correlation. Once we tap into the alignment of the chakras and activate the pineal, energy becomes more profound from a spiritual perspective. We are a spiritual vibrating energy field creating that which is, and that which is to be. It has become clear that we are part of the universe, and this universal law governs natural phenomena; it becomes clear that the universe is tightly welded to manifest anything we desire. The chakras and the glands are synonymous and provide an avenue to activate the light energy of the body. The crown chakra is the pineal gland, the brow or third eye chakra is the pituitary gland, the throat chakra is the thyroid gland, the heart chakra is the thymus gland, the solar plexus is the pancreas gland, the sacral chakra is the ovaries gland, and the root chakra is the adrenal gland. Light energy is activated when all the glands and chakras are consistently aligned and grounded.

CHAPTER 4:
MEDITATION AND RELAXATION

Chakras and Alignment

Now that we have followed through on the symmetry of the body, brain, and nervous system to realize its importance in activating and grounding the body, mind, and soul, we will move on to one of my favorite subjects, chakra alignment. How do we get the body ready for meditation and relaxation? I pose this question with one answer: alignment of the chakras. When we align the chakras, the law of attraction is obtainable to anyone trying to manifest their dreams. When the chakras are aligned, the body reacts to the right karma that is suitable for the right situations that may occur at a particular and specific time. Nothing comes out of the blue; everything is karma. Focus on karma, expand your vibrating energy, single out thoughts, feelings, and actions, and track them into your life for success.

Chakra alignments occur with the activation of the spinal cord, which connects the nervous system, thus slowing down or speeding up the vibrational frequency. Our nervous system generates electricity, and the polarity of the spirits and body gives rise to the magnetic field surrounding the body in the form of your aura. When we can strive for perfection by aligning the chakras, we activate the lost senses, track material information to accomplish our desires, and turn our dreams into reality. Chakra alignments may create an enhanced magnetic field around the body. Your body is attracting and manifesting the things you need, the people you need, the knowledge you need, and the energy you need for action.

We can now see why the body is like an antenna, and the pineal gland is the gateway to activate higher frequencies.

Chakra alignment activates the melanin in the pineal gland, stimulating sound, color, and the points of the nervous system.

There are points along the chakras to be activated and aligned with the spinal and nervous systems for certain ventures. Each of the electromagnetic entities along the spinal cord has its own frequencies, its own rhythm of pulsation, and its own sounds. The body is a natural semiconductor that attracts what you desire when activated; one can speak those substances into existence. You are the artificial intelligence when you activate and align your chakras. The chakras are the electrodes and points that enhance the vibration of the nervous system. By aligning the chakras, you create, enhance, and provide a positive aura around the body. Look at it this way: our nervous system generates electricity as a current of sounds, colors, and feelings through the body and mind. This current reacts with the magnetic field around the body. When the body frequencies are in harmony with the earth's frequencies, it enhances the body's ions, which produces relaxation and meditation.

When we align the chakras, we align our bodies with the universal law of attraction from a vibration perspective. These universal laws are divine laws associated with your divine image. When the body is aligned with the chakras, the divine laws tap into the inner well-being, creating resistance. This is when we allow things to let go; resistance helps us let go of anxiety, fear, struggle, and lack. We can find the simple truth presented in the alpha state for more relaxation. Meditation and relaxation are more profound when we align and activate the seven chakras. There are seven primary axes on the spinal cord that need to be activated: the pineal gland, the brow (third eye), the throat, the heart, the adrenal (solar plexus), the sacral, and the gonads. We start the alignment process by using the seven harmonic sounds through vibrations to communicate with the creators. *"But know that the Lord has set apart him that is Godly for himself; the Lord will hear when I call."*

Use of Mantra (earth sounds, musical tones)

Buddhist monks have used the mantra sounds for thousands of years to reach a higher spiritual awakening. Using these mantra sounds, earth sounds, or musical sounds is a way to activate the chakras; these mantra sounds appear to soothe the inner spirits and communicate with the god within. When each sound is used in its proper place, it raises the vibratory frequency and activates the attribute associated with that gland. Some of the mantras sound carry significant meanings and spiritual values. For instance, the etiologic root word Aum is taken from the Sumerian text, Atum, as in Atum Re. Amum, as in Amen-Re, the raising of the sun rays, as in Genesis 1:3: God says, let there be light, and John 1:4: and the light was the spark of life that shone in the darkness. Aum is the awakening of the first chakras; the crown is the top of the head that signifies the elector ruler. Concentrating on the crown and repeating the sound aum-m-m-m-m-m-m-m-m-m can create a feeling of euphoria. When entering the crown, the sound aum raises the vibrations that promote intellectual awakening and send the chemicals endorphin and serotonin to the brain.

The sound om—m-m-m-m-m-m-m vibrates at a rate that allows each energy field, with the consciousness, to create molecules that make up its body frequencies. These frequencies flow across the body's membranes to magnify forced energy and allow the aura to flow freely. Although we have different sounds, each organ system is composed of cells with the same harmony with nature and the body. The sound Om is considered by Hindu scripture as the primordial sound of the universe. For instance, each liver, heart, blood, and spleen cell is activated in tune with the universe. When you continue to repeat the sound om, it awakens and activates the pineal gland and the brow or the third eye, promoting a sense of spiritual awakening of the four additional senses: clairvoyance, telepathy, intuition, and psychometry.

The hum sound is represented in the universe and symbolizes the fact that all humans are interconnected. The hum sound activates the throat chakra, which controls the body's metabolic rates and converts food into energy. The thyroid and parathyroid glands are associated with physical growth and are believed to affect one's mental development. The throat chakra is linked with all forms of communication and correspondence and balance rationale, approach, and emotional expressions. The way we speak is the way we communicate with our peers, colleagues, and the spirit world. The humming sound makes it clear that we are speaking of that which we adhere to and see into existence. Did not God speak the world into existence?

Yum - m-m-m-m-m-m-m-m-m-m-m-m-m-m-m-m, yum, although not considered a universal sound, still carries significance when activating the chakras. The sound yum activates the heart chakra and is the lifeguard of the body, mind, and soul. It is closely related to vital organs such as the lungs, liver, and lymphatic system. When activated, it promotes health and balance in the body.

The sound Ram-m-m-m-m-m-m-m is the sound for the solar plexus center or adrenal glands. While everything centers around the sun, everything physical centers around the adrenal glands or solar plexus. When premonition, intuition, or wrong feeling occurs, you often feel it in this body area. It is called a gut feeling.

The vam sound is considered the seat of the soul center of the cells of the lymphatic system. This chakra-sacral-internal organ gives intuitive energy. It is the cradle of the spleen, found in the abdomen next to the stomach, behind the lower rib.

Finally, the lam sound, the base of the spine, or the gonads. To activate this area of the body is called grounding. When we ground, activating the chakras, we start at the base of the spine, radiating the sound down the legs into the earth's walls.

For effect, repeat each mantra three times for each center. Start at the crown chakra and move down. Let the chakras spin one way, going down, and spin the opposite way, coming up the spine. We can also use musical notes: DO, RE, ME, FA, SO. LA, TI, with their representative colors.

Use of Color Power

When we activate the chakras, we enhance and release hormones to the body's vital organs for ultimate health, maintaining our physiological cycles, controlling our digestive system, managing our emotions, and regulating our body temperature. We are activating the pineal gland, the pituitary gland, the thyroid gland, the pancreas gland, the ovaries, and the adrenal glands. Activating the chakras allows us to convert energy into motion to meet our true god self; the spiritual self, the god in man, begins to manifest itself. Repeating the mantra through each chakra is an excellent way to reach the alpha state for balance and meditation. As mentioned above, we can also use musical sound notes with colors to enhance our ability to visualize and manifest our desires into reality.

Let us review the chakra points on the spinal cord: the pineal, the pituitary, the thyroid, the heart or thymus, the adrenals, the Leydig (sacral), and the gonads. We will associate each chakra with its color, musical note sound, and universal sound for maximum effects and visualization meditations.

Red violet, purple, or violet are associated with the crown chakra, the pineal gland. The musical sound is DO, and its universal sound is Am-m-m-m-m-m; the color red-violet activates self-actualization, enhances the energy related to the cerebral cortex, and promotes creativity, scientific exploration, intuitive power, and the desire for humanitarian activities. The musical sound DO helps signify the release of hormones that stimulate a response to stress and growth, manage and activate energy from food, enhance the reproductive system, and promote lactation for female milk.

Indigo is associated with the chakra of the pituitary gland, which is concentrated between the brow and the third eye of the soul, emitting and creating energy portals. The musical sound is RE; when repeated, with its universal sound Um-m-m-m-m-m, while visualizing the color indigo, it recreates intuitive impulses that create the need for achievement. Visualizing the color indigo, repeating RE also activates and produces the hormone melatonin responsible for skin color and hair pigmentation. Special care is given when activating this brain area because of its spiritual dynamics.

Blue is associated with the throat chakra, signifying the need for effective communication. When we visualize blue on this chakra, utilizing the sound MI and the mantra Hum-m-m-m-m-m creates a desire for increased self-esteem. We are regulating the thyroid gland in front of the neck and the parathyroid gland behind the thyroid gland. The MI and the universal Hum sounds increase the calcium level in the blood and control metabolism, creating the impulses that demand the need and respect of others.

Green is associated with the heart chakra, the circular energy center. When activated, it emits energy that translates into a desire for love and socialization. To activate the heart chakra, imagine inhaling the color green and, when exhaling, make a soft sound of the musical note fa. Because the heart has its own consciousness, it also begins to create steroid hormones that could be adrenaline or non-adrenaline. Adrenaline regulates and controls heart rate, blood pressure, and stress hormones.

Yellow is the pancreas chakra, the solar plexus; its relationship is to shelter, protection, and nurturing. The musical sound associated with the pancreas chakras is SO, and when you utilize the musical sound SO, or the mantra sound Rum-r-r-r-r-r with yellow, it activates the vibration of the solar plexus. The solar plexus is the center of the body and, by medical definition, is named the celiac plexus. The celiac plexus is found in the pit of the stomach and can easily be shut down. This chakra, unlike the other four, is part of the sympathetic nervous system. The solar plexus deals with emotions, where you often hear the term gut feeling. To activate the solar plexus, visualize yellow and chant the musical note SO; this practice will give you a sense of personal power, knowledge, and intuition. When activated with yellow and the musical note SOL, this chakra will also give you a sense of caring, promote a strong impulse of protection, and create the need for shelter.

Understanding Light Energy

Earlier, we discussed light energy, its effect on the body, and how we can control and activate the energy surrounding it. Hence, we emphasize that the body may indeed act as a superconductor moving through time, space, and dimension. The body we know is in constant vibrations with the earth, the solar system, and the universe. While we are vibrating, we give out thermal energy to the universe, and the universe provides that which we mostly focus on in our thought process. This energy field is in tune with our subconscious mind and produces our good or bad lifestyle. However, we must be in a relaxed state of mind with the light. We can be assured that we can create our just desires by understanding a few principles of the body. We are the created force of all things, and a system that is systematic in nature. We are constantly dealing with our counterparts on a spiritual plane and the plane of the force of light. On this energy force, we start with the plane of hydrogen H, onto Einsteinium, the 99th element, and then move to man-made elements, fermium, mendelevium, nobelium, and lawrencium.

This energy force light is an etheric realm, starting with ether one, going back through the 99 ethers, making the energy in reverse and of a different nature; however, the etheric realm is beyond the element realms. The etheric realm is where we find our DNA, constantly revolving, and its chief function is to create energy for cellular activity, which consists of protons, which have a positive charge, and neutrons, which have no charge; they are called nucleons. These protons and neutrons are the nucleus of the cells found in the mitochondria. DNA is inherited from our mothers. When studying neutrons, we will see that neutrons are uncharged particles and one of the fundamental particles of matter. Free neutrons are constituent particles of all nuclei, and those outside of atomic nuclei are produced in nuclear reactions. They can be ejected from atomic nuclei at various speeds or energies and are readily slowed down to very low energy by a series of collisions with light nuclei.

The body comprises approximately thirty-three million cells transmitting and receiving bioelectrical energy. These cells comprise ionic electrolytes that hydrate, energize, and produce chemicals such as potassium, calcium, and magnesium. To further understand the light energy of the body, scientists have discovered that lithium extends cell life and human life span by stimulating the production of something called a telomere, an anti-aging enzyme responsible for promoting cellular health and life extension. These high-conductivity ionic electrolytes need alkalinity liquids and minerals to survive the acidic stomach digestion system for natural balance. However, I propose that activating the chakras provides a natural balance, enhancing light energy to help the body improve focus, clarity, memory, and mood. Activating the chakras may enhance the chemical process of the brain to protect neurons from toxins and elevate frequency.

Affirmation To Enhance Your Meditations

According to Merriam-Webster Dictionary's new edition, affirmation is to confirm, assert positively, and make a solemn and formal declaration or assertion in place of an oath. Conversely, Google states that affirmation is the action or process of affirming something or being affirmed, or emotional support or encouragement. The root word is "process." In other words, affirmation is a process of confirming something that you want to happen, and it is something that you perform consistently. I have considered several quotes I have used to affirm my daily meditation practices.

Consider these quotes: *"Every problem must be seen as an opportunity to realize the God in you for growth and development,"* or *"Don't let the past cover your future; each moment is a fresh new moment, an opportunity to change, grow, and begin again."*

"Releasing the past, letting go is not about having the courage to release the past; it is about having the wisdom to embrace the present."

Steve Maraboli

It is easy to reach the alpha state of consciousness when activating the seven chakras, using the seven universal sounds, or tones, with the seven sun colors. Once you have learned to reach the alpha state using this technique, your state of mind will become calm, your body will be more relaxed, and meditation will be more achievable. Choose the affirmation that is relevant to your present situation and repeat your affirmation after each section. Your vibration will slowly rise, the problem will become clearer, and the solution will appear before your eyes. One thing I have learned about using affirmation with meditation is that you hardly know it is working until it has been completed. Affirmation works similarly to prayers; it has no effect on the unbeliever. Consider Mark 11:24 of the Holy Bible: "Therefore I say unto you, all things, whatsoever you ask when you pray, believe that you shall receive, and they shall come unto you."

These ten affirmations of gratefulness have worked wonders in my life and helped me to sustain a healthy lifestyle. I don't take them lightly, and share them because I know they have worked for me and will work for you as well:

(1) I am grateful to be alive, healthy, and with a sound mind;

(2) I am grateful for my family and that they are healthy and well;

(3) I am grateful for the many monies and finances that have manifested in my life;

(4) I am grateful for the success that I have obtained, my education, writing my first book, and receiving a large amount of money in royalties;

(5) I am grateful for the beautiful home the universe has provided to my family and me;

(6) I am grateful for the wonderful car, clothing, furniture, and pleasures of life the universe has provided for me;

(7) I am grateful the creator has allowed me to help hundreds, if not thousands, of my fellow humans and their families with my wisdom;

(8) I am grateful to have served my people;

(9) I am grateful for the breath of life, and living amongst the living;

(10) I am grateful and thankful for the universe giving me favor in the eyes of my peers, thanking the creator for opening my eyes to my purpose in life. I am thankful for the creator, the God of the universe, and the God in me. Atum, Atom, Amen.

CHAPTER 5:
RELAXATION THERAPY

The Alpha State of Mind

We can activate the complete deep breathing system to help us reach the alpha state much sooner for relaxation and meditation. Complete deep breathing techniques allow the maximum amount of air to replenish blood cells, which will help relieve stress, anxiety, and depression. We look at our daily lives as having many duties and responsibilities that often overwhelm us and cause stress. We can take three completely deep, refreshing breaths while sitting in our office or waiting for a job interview. It will only take a few minutes to relax, move into the alpha state, reach the unconscious mind, and correct negative thoughts and views. It is most likely that the subconscious mind is the culprit, causing distress in the thought pattern, therefore throwing off the chemical balance of serotonin and endorphins in the brain. We can bring these chemicals back into balance. Our body will automatically relax, and our magnetic field will change, and we will be able to raise the frequency and control the subconscious.

A simple way to destroy doubt in the subconscious mind is to relax. Using the complete deep breathing system makes deep breathing a relaxing task. Stress, anxiety, and worries can be gone. This will activate the hidden power of God in you; you must first learn how to relax. The complete deep breathing technique is a simple way to get into an alpha state for relaxation and to release stress.

When you relax, you may recognize the positive and negative talk in the subconscious mind; we want to recognize and eliminate this by taking control of our thought process. When we control our breathing, we can recognize the negative and positive thoughts that activate the chemical endocrine and other fluids that create anxiety, stress, and depression. Recognizing negative thoughts, eliminating them, and sending positive thoughts to the mind primes the positivity pump program of the brain. The complete deep breathing technique can assist the most anxious person with negative self-talk.

Let us review this exercise: find a comfortable position with your legs uncrossed, hand at your side, or placed on your lap. Close your eyes and take a deep, complete breath. Use the four counts to ensure you are using the complete breathing technique. Feel the air moving into the nostrils; feel the stomach moving out; feel the diaphragm moving up and feel the lungs filling with air; hold for the count of four, then release the carbon dioxide slowly at the count of four, feeling the stomach going back in. Be conscious that you are not exhaling through your mouth. Some teach us to breathe through our mouths, which is fine, but we want to obtain the maximum amount of air to the cells. Take another deep, complete breath, filling the lungs, and hold for the count of four, but when exhaling and using the four counts, visualize the number four as well. When we visualize the number four, we tell the subconscious that we are taking control, now relaxing the body. Take another deep, complete breath, filling the lungs completely, holding for the count of four, but this time, while releasing the breath, say to yourself, "*I am quite calm. My breathing is calm; my breathing is regular---I am quite well---nothing can distract me---I am totally relaxed---my arms, legs, and shoulders are flexible and relaxed---I am breathing slowly, regularly, ---with each breath, I sink into this deep, peaceful, pleasant sensation or relaxation and love.*" Just sit for a few minutes and notice any new or negative thoughts; let them be, and do not try to discard them. Relax for a few minutes and enjoy the peace and relaxation. Always come out of your three relaxation breaths with the four-countdown process. Count backward with the four-count method: four, feel your body losing; three, feel your shoulder becoming lighter; two, feel your face getting brighter; and one, open your eyes.

Control the Subconscious Mind with the Four Eighth Count

When we understand that breathing is the key component we use for deep relaxation and meditation, we understand the life cycle of God in humans. The importance of breathing correctly cannot be understated. It is the most important thing we will focus on throughout this text. Without proper breathing, it is impossible to control the subconscious mind. The millisecond that the subconscious recognizes that you are out of turn with your breathing, it will control, take back control, cause chaos with your thought process, and control your very thoughts and actions. If at all one could have complete control of the subconscious mind, then they would be geniuses, God on Earth. However, we have the God in us, and breathing correctly draws us closer to that genius within us. When we become consistent with recognizing our breathing in tune with nature and the magnetic fields, we can immediately take control of our subconscious mind and manifest our will.

In some of the ancient Sumerian texts, it was written that the Sumerians held the most importance in breathing; breath is life itself, and nothing exists without breath (Shu). Shu is an ancient Tama-Re name that means "uplifter, to uplift oneself." Written in hieroglyphs on the wall of (Kemet) Egypt in the old writing, the name Shu signifies life, growth, vegetation, and the provider of sustenance to the sustained physical body. Shu is the air and breath that trigger the ether through proper breathing that controls the subconscious mind. Air is scary to the body and controls the vibration and intonation to bring one into a spiritual world; air is spiritual. People all over the world have identified air with spirit.

In addition, the brain, the catalyst and most powerful access to activate God, needs proper amounts of air. The brain comprises billions of nerves needing air to nourish them, and each neuron in the brain is equivalent to 60 megabits of RAM. Henceforth, they can process thousands of thoughts per minute. Therefore, when activated by air-to-fuel chemicals, the brain is used to visualize thoughts in the subconscious mind. Unlike a placebo effect experiment--when a person believes that they have been given something that eases their symptoms if they believe that the placebo is working--it releases all the symptoms. If left alone and done repetitively, the mind will slowly believe that it has happened and become a reality. We activate the subconscious mind to create what we believe is our reality.

We want to live as much as possible in the alpha state of mind to monitor and control the subconscious mind. We want to practice the deep, complete breath techniques constantly, but this time, we will use the four-eight count.

Find a comfortable position, close your eyes, and relax your body using the four, by four, by four method. Once you have reached the alpha state of mind, sit still for several seconds. Next, take complete breaths at the count of four; do not hold, and release at the count of eight. Three quick breaths is one rotation; perform three rotations and repeat the following statement: *"The law of attraction is orchestrating and attracting all that I need. My thoughts, feelings, and actions track and manifest what I desire. My thoughts and vibrations are connected to all universal laws, allowing things to happen within my inner being, releasing resistance, letting go of anxiety, fear, struggle, and lack. My subconscious mind no longer has control; it is the simple truth. I am now attracting joy, happiness, or abundance; my body is in harmony and balance, creating ultimate health and prosperity."* To receive the optimal benefits from this exercise, repeat the four/eight count, sit still for eight counts after each rotation, and then slowly open your eyes.

When we are performing relaxation therapy, we are streamlining the mental process of the subconscious mind, which has accumulated hours of news and media information for months and years. We are simply bringing the subconscious mind back to present reality.

"Sharpen your eyes, tune your ears, so you will know what you see and understand what you hear."

Socrates

Using These Power Source Statements

"From the origin of things is to know thyself."

Socrates

When a person streamlines their thought process through meditation, they bring their subconscious mind under subjection. This unique science of the body is living and residing within you. When you relax and meditate, you open up your spiritual mindset. Once the spiritual mindset is open, you will want to fill it with prayer, affirmations, or gratitude statements. When you use a source statement, you acknowledge with words that there is truly source energy, or God energy, more powerful than you, radiating and creating your life. Acknowledging the existence of God in a person helps build blocks for confidence that there is a faithful god source. When you realize that universal laws are interacting with the electromagnetic vibration of your body to create substance, you can understand how important words and statements are when trying to create your reality.

For a closer look at the concept of how important statements are to the mindset, we read the statements of Yeshua in Matthew 7: 7-8:

"Ask, and it shall be given you; seek, and you shall find; knock, and it shall be opened unto you; for everyone that asked receives; and he that seeketh findeth; and to him that knocketh it shall be opened."

None of this will happen if we disregard Matthew 7:11-12:

"If you then, being evil, know how to give good gifts unto your children, how much more shall your Father, which is in heaven, give good things to them that ask him?"

And Matthew 7-12:

"Therefore, all things whatsoever you would that men should do to you, do you even so to them; for this is the law and the prophets."

We must have the God-like characteristics to accomplish any task we have at hand. Wouldn't letting the God in you help manifest what you desire be nice? Wouldn't you like to build that characteristic by using breathing exercises, relaxing, and studying while developing a God-like character? By reading positive attributes and affirmations, you are doing just that.

There are many affirmations and positive quotes found on the internet that can assist you in developing a Godly mindset. I will share a few on the page, read them with confidence, weary not, and notice the results of your character and attitudes.

- Every problem must be seen as an opportunity for growth and development.

- There is a God-like vacuum within us. (Rev Ike)

- Those who have based their foundation on their revelation find joy, hope, and peace of mind.

- You are the image of God and the result of millions of years of evolution.

- "What is a disaster for most is an opportunity for few." (Richard Ney)

- When you find your main objective, quick and easy ways to visualize and manifest appear,

- To produce joy, hope, wealth, and peace of mind is your birthright.

- You must activate the God in you to promote becoming the God in you.

- Access your strengths and weaknesses and create a clear assessment of your desired goals.

- Upload your body vibrations for success and gain favoritism with the God within.

- 'God will provide all your needs according to his riches in glory: (Philippians 4::14)

- To control the unconscious mind, align the body with the God within and reality without.

- Create a clear and descriptive picture given by God within to activate actions.

- Those who base their belief on a loving God, act in their behest, and create an image in the best interest of others and themselves, tend to bring their desires into reality (Kurt Tepper Wein)

- To obtain the desired results, create an inspirational alignment with the God that is in you.

- "You must have a clear position; you cannot agree on what you are in disagreement with, because of the irreconcilable differences, there is no real desire to manifest."

- Your desires must be in agreement, and your goals must embrace the supportive will of God and his mutual benefits.

- Success or failure is in the thoughts produced by the unconscious mind.

- Material manifestation begins once the thoughts are spoken to the conscious mind.

- Life (success and death (failure) are in the power of the tongue (Prov. 18:21) (22). Problems are solved by recognizing God, your source, and the God in you, you-affirming your beliefs in the source, and yourself.

Grateful Statement to Live By

"This is the Lord your redeemer, The Holy One of Israel; I am the Lord your God, who teaches you to profit, who leads you the way you should go."

Isaiah 48:17.

You must be committed and clear about where you want to go, and what you want to do and become. Furthermore, you must understand how to be grateful for where you are today, right now, while focusing on what tomorrow looks like for you. You are tailoring a clear road to your destination when your vision is open and modified. Your vision and your dreams will begin to materialize. Ask yourself, Are you grateful for what you have right now? Or are you unsatisfied with where you are in life? If you are reading this text right now, you are right where you must be in life, so be graceful.

When you have an unresolved plan, and the vision is clear and obtainable, give thanks. To understand the existence of God in you, the vision of God in you, the soul of God in you, the spirit of God in you, and the intelligence of God in you, give thanks. Every situation must be seen as an opportunity to realize the growth and development of your plan. Be thankful. Each time you use the complete breathing system for relaxation and meditation, align your chakras, use the seven earth sounds, and visualize the seven major colors, you bring your body into subjection with God. Be thankful that you could sit and perform these exercises with ease. Your visualization becomes clearer; you can recognize and take advantage of the opportunities that appear before you. Be graceful and know that you have come this far in life to continue your quest for knowledge and unique power. Every day, when you give grace, living becomes more gracious. When you say you are grateful for what you have and for how you feel, it activates the vital substance for peace and tranquility.

When we say we are grateful, the universe lifts our vibrations for universal awareness and spiritual guidance. We are not just saying thank you. We are saying that we have the courage, the energy, and the confidence to go forward with this day toward our quest. You're the kingdom of the universe, heaven, and the earth. You can do all things, the God in you; you are living right now in majesty; you are thankful that you were created in the image of God and the likeness of a creator. You are creating your reality and are able to do great things, and you are grateful that you are moving forward with confidence.

The science of the body is uniquely electromagnetic, spiritual, and intelligent. The body is unique to God, the creator, or your source energy, residing within you to do great things. When we recognize the God within us, we recognize that we can move to new heights of success. Therefore, we prioritize and place the source of our endeavor first, the God within, in a gracefully, pure, actionable, and godly manner. Therefore, give your God, source energy, provider, and spirituality the glory.

Be still and recognize the power of God within (normalize your thoughts); let your thoughts be good. When we are grateful for what we have and our health, our soul grows inwardly through its inner senses and ages of enlightenment and wisdom.

We genuinely recognize that what we are grateful for manifests in our dreams, visions, and desires.

The Power of Prayer

"I command thee be strong and of good courage; be not afraid, neither be dismayed; for the created thy God is with you whitherever thou goest."

Joshua 1-9

Humble thyself to the creator and the creator within. The tremendous power source, the most gracious, the most precious, and the most powerful. The master of all things, the universe, the earth, the planets, the sun, the moon, and everything in them is. I believe that we are not immortals. Still, we can use the subconscious's objective parts to manifest what we desire through visualizing and affirming our existence.

The subconscious mind is the god within you and is responsible for everything it produces. The God-man is different from the physical; it is your spirit. We are both physical and spiritual. The source of energy you create comes from within you. You make the image manifest within your world. When we pray, we build our spiritual world within us. We have faith within us that what we prayed for is already done. We pray to reach deep within the subconscious mind to acknowledge that what we speak will come to pass.

CHAPTER 6:
ACTIVATE THE POWER OF VISUALIZATION AND DREAM

Dreams and Sleep Patterns

Reaching the true spirit of God in you through prayer is referenced in most biblical texts and used as a formal way to communicate with the prophets. When we study the Torah, the first five chapters of the Holy Bible, we read that God communicates with Abraham through visions and dreams. In Genesis 15:1, you'll find an example. He did this to test Abraham's comfort and confidence. We will have many dreams and visions of success throughout our lifespan, but we will not recognize them, and we will accomplish very few. Our dreams fly right by and away from us without us knowing. Years later, we see the same ideal we had thought of in our dream become a reality with someone else's invention. Your dreams and sleep patterns are tools to recognize and act on quickly, and to continue visualizing and acting on until those dreams become your reality. When you begin to realize your dreams and visions, it is easier to incorporate them into your daily meditation routine and daily life. Begin using the deep, complete breathing methods, relaxing the body, aligning the chakras, and visualizing your dream and vision after God has sent you a dream in your sleep.

When you journalize your dreams, you utilize your intellectual and intuitive abilities. You begin to recognize that things materialize because you activate Source energy. Ultimately, with a daily practice of meditation, visualization, and recognizing dreams becomes part of your reality. You will become dedicated and committed to realizing your dreams and visions. You will be more determined to block out and not let fear and doubt rule your dimensions. Your confidence continues to build, and you gain more perseverance until your goals are reached and your dreams and visions give you material gain. Once you see your dreams and visions materialize, the experience of accomplishment will bring joy, peace, and prosperity.

You must face the fact early on that no one will give you anything; no matter what the dream or the vision is, you will have to create a team and put forth effort to reach your goals. You do not want your dreams and visions to become just a fantasy; you want to see daily progress. When you plant the first objectives in your guide, make the objectives easily obtainable during the initial process. When you gain your first taste of victory, you will get the taste of manifesting; this is the feeling you want to keep throughout the process. The goals are the roots that grow into achievements. Goals cannot be achieved without discipline (watering) and consistency (positive effort). When you dream or visualize your desires, good and moral, they can be accomplished. Anything you want that is good, you can have, so claim it, work each day diligently toward those goals, and when you reach it, reach back and pull someone else up with you.

When you have a clear picture of your visualization, eliminate anything in the dream that is negative and unproductive. Correct things in the dreams you feel are unpleasant, and manifest things that are good and straightforward. Journalizing your dream life is not a portion of your desires, but the picture becomes viable with more and better things. Therefore, you want to see wellness, you want to see yourself being successful, and you want to see yourself loving and being loved. See yourself prosper and joyful; see yourself wealthy and debt-free. Visualizing it clears your mind of all negative aspects except what you want to manifest. It would be best if you decided clearly what you want; visualization helps you organize those thoughts. When you master the art of visualization, you may be capable of creating a deep connection with the subconscious mind. Your images will become apparent, colorful, and organized, leaving you with encouragement and motivation.

When you visualize your dream, you must have the propensity to associate with successful people, learning and growing from them. It is worth remembering when visualizing your dream that the law of the mind has no respect for a person, so choose wisely. The opposing suggestion of your visualization in a dream can be an opposing force that can become a mental block to your success. Moreover, when visualizing, seeing your progression becomes a level of mind that doesn't necessarily deal with reason; things begin to come from a spiritual concept, and you recognize the God within.

Daytime Dreaming and Visualization

It is often taught that your reason cannot be imagined, and your imagination cannot reason. Therefore, work with your imagination when visualizing, and simultaneously with your reasoning. Your visualization and dreams result from the inner mind, the God within. You must build the imagination in the inner person and let it become a part of you. When you are fascinated with what you want to be, do, and have, your visualization and dreams become a reality. You see yourself having, being, and doing what you desire before it becomes a reality.

Have you ever been out and about early in the morning, shopping or doing some chores? Because there is so little traffic at that time of day, you see a green Ferrari speed by you, pipes loud, music blasting, and then it's gone. You just saw your dream car flash in front of your face and go just as quickly. Your imagination or your daydream. Have you gotten lost and caught up in a strange neighborhood with large mansions, beautiful landscapes, and luxury cars parked in the driveway? Another daydream? We are always daydreaming or lost in thought when we see something that resembles our dreams. For just that split moment, your visualization becomes a reality, and you see, feel, and smile at what it's like to live in that dream. Does it give you confidence when you have these types of experiences? What is your feeling? What is your motivation?

When you practice the relaxation, meditation, and visualizations shown in this text, you will activate the hidden power of God in you, you will begin to recognize and see your dreams with clarity, and you will have activated the true nine senses connected to the source. When you have a scene where you see what you have dreamed about, the nine senses are open to you for the benefit of accomplishing your vision. What was the experience, you ask? Visualizing, seeing it in reality; audio-duction, hearing the sounds; gustation, tasting the air; olfaction, smelling the fumes from the engine of the Ferrari; tac-tuition, touching the steering wheel, feeling, and smelling the leather in the past car; your vibration has been rising to a higher frequency. Premonition is present in the future while you live it now; telepathy thrusts you into communicating in the now reality; intuition can understand the psychic of something without reason; teleporting has been placed into this time, for this reason, and has communicated through transformation.

Have you ever stayed awake at night thinking about what your dream vacation would look like? Imagine getting all of what you have visualized, dreamed, and talked about. Capture the excitement of horseback riding in the Caribbean or join a handful of people to swim with the dolphins in the Cayman Islands. Imagine it on your next break or while folding the laundry. Daydream now and often, and see your reality materialize before your face. Your dreams and sleep patterns unlock the unconscious and help you find the hidden power of God in you.

Relaxation Technique Before Going to Sleep

When discussing relaxation and its different techniques, we discuss exchanging air and carbon dioxide, nurturing and fueling the brain and body. When performing the complete deep breathing technique, you exchange the body and air, acid-base balance, regulation, phonation, and nervous system, and initiate the bioelectrical frequency of the body. When you activate the central nervous system, it interacts with and responds to your behavior and environment, controlling the function of your organs and your subconscious mind. Meditating and using relaxation techniques are the same, whether performed after getting up in the morning or before going to bed at night. Because our mind has taken on every visible negative thing during the day, it may have become foggy from abstract scenery not necessary to our initial goals or benefits. Instead of relaxing the body, we want to focus more on the mind at night and ensure it is calm before sleep.

You may have just come home from work or picked up the children from daycare, but you are tired and would like a few seconds to slow down your mind, not minutes. Take one deep, complete breath and let it out slowly. It only takes thirty seconds. You do not need much time to do this technique because you will take this deep breath every hour when you think of it. Each time you take this deep breath, you release all the clutter from whatever negatively happened that day. By the time you have completed all chores for the evening, sit somewhere quietly and take a deep breath, and while exhaling, count backward from thirty to zero. When performing the deep breathing technique and counting from 30 to zero, do not try to remember any thoughts; just let the thoughts move freely out of your subconscious mind. Concentrate on your breathing and nothing else. When you are ready for bed, lie down and take three profound breaths, with each breath counting backward from sixty to zero three times, then go to sleep. Each time you awake throughout the night, repeat the process.

If you practice this technique consistently for two or three weeks, you will add more hours to your sleep. You will begin to dream again, like when you were younger. Your dreams will become more vivid and clear. Try to differentiate between your imagination and your dreams. Understand that your imagination can become flawed and seem more like a nightmare, whereas your dream will be more of what you desire. When you perform the complete deep breathing technique with the countdown backward method, you activate the God within to clean the house and give you something new in the environment to respond to.

Journalize Your Dreams. They Become Your Vision Board

According to Merriam-Webster's Dictionary, a journal is a brief account of daily events, a record of proceedings, and a periodical dealing with current events. When you journalize, you will not be recording daily events, only using the journal to jot down clues to your dreams. Keep the journal by the night light on your nightstand. You will only use the journal from your relaxation and meditation sections when you have a suspicion, intuition, or out-of-body experience. Before you journalize your dreams, ensure you have perfected the relaxation techniques for sleep. After you perform the sleep relaxation technique, ask your source energy, your God, or your God within to reveal the interpretation of your hunch, intuition, or out-of-body experience in a dream. When your Source reveals to you, in your dream, that which you asked for, wake up immediately after the dream and jot down anything that you can remember about the dream.

We often allow fear to interfere with what we most desire. We miss the picture designed within our dreams when we are not disciplined enough to relax and meditate. Also, we fear patience, most often striving for instant gratification. Meditation creates a mindset for us to gain patience. Meditation also releases stress and anxiety. When we hold on to fear and apprehension, we are creating an illusory world. Most often, a lack of planning will cause anxiety and hinder our actions to pursue our goals. Before preparing your journal, relax deeply, activate the seven chakras, meditate, and visualize what you desire. In your visualization stage, outline a specific action plan for your desired goals. Be sure to write them down in your visualization state of mind instead of just visualizing them. Create an outline and write the first three items that come to mind that you can do tomorrow. Plan to complete the task. When you complete the first task on your outline, your confidence will be built immediately. You will slowly gain more confidence in yourself, and fear will slowly dissipate. Try to perform this visualization exercise at night before bed, and keep a journal on your nightstand to assist you in memorizing certain specific details of your dream.

When you begin to journalize your dream, you are actually creating a vision board that is very attainable and suitable for the goals you have set for yourself. When you begin to journalize your dreams, you create a partnership with your subconscious mind, becoming the gatekeeper while you are sleeping. You can record these actions and put them into play in the conscious state. You do not have any more fear, doubt, or apprehension that your dream is being lived in the present after you have written it down.

Your Vision and Thoughts Become Your Reality

When you start waking up throughout the night and journalizing your dreams, your vision and thoughts become your reality. You have awakened the God, the source, the alpha within. You begin to see your new world manifest in front of your eyes; the journey becomes more of an adventure instead of a performing task. The principles of the frequencies, the subconscious, the conscious, and vibrations in tune with the earth produce your results. You are beginning to ascend to the God-like person you were made to be, and have your desires.

You ascend into the manifestation, where every good deed always produces an award. Your faith strengthens, your belief becomes more achievable, and you are happier with your life and where you live now. You become more grateful for all you have and continue to gain more. In your new reality, you realize there is no such thing as debt; only assets, property, and capital exist. The more you understand that your new world is overflowing with abundance, the more the creator and the God within will allow. Whatever state you are in right now, you know that abundance is plenty, and you have access to it. Worries, doubts, and insecurity have vanished. Your goals are clear and specific, and your mindset is programmed for actionable results.

Alter your life by altering your attitude, using positive words and phrases in your journal, and every so often using one of your favorite quotes or scripture. "If you can believe, all things are possible to them who believe." (Mark 9:23). See yourself where you want to be within the next five years. See the homes, see the cars, see yourself traveling, see the clothing, see the money, the success, the wealth, and the health. Your reward will always be an exact proportion of your contribution to your service.

Our vision must be clear and specific about what we want to manifest before activating the God within our source. "I am the Lord your God, who teaches you to profit, who leads you the way you should go." (Isaiah 48-17) Be very clear about what you so desire. When we open our chakras and activate our clairvoyance, a clear vision allowing us to see things that are not in sight or cannot be seen, we have a keen insight to use. Our vision becomes a road map of our destination and what the destination result looks like. You have been practicing the complete breathing techniques, you have been using your relaxation techniques, you have been aligning the seven chakras, performing the seven mantras, and activating the seven colors, you have been visualizing your dream life, journalizing your dreams, and now bringing into universal awareness the realization of any solution that may come for in real life for your manifestations.

"Put your shoes way under the bed at night; for you to get your shoes when you wake up, you have to get on your knees, so while you are down there, pray and be grateful for what you have."

Denzel Washington.

"Anything that you want that is good, you can have it, so claim it, work hard to get it, and when you get it, reach back and pull someone else up."

Maya Angelou.

CHAPTER 7:
ACTIVATE THE GOD WITHIN WITH HYPNOSIS

Law of Attractions

The purpose of activating the seven chakras is to raise your thoughts to infinite wisdom to attract what is seen in the inner conscious. When you activate the seven chakras, you want to visualize the seven significant colors and imagine the color for each chakra entering that particular chakra. Now, transcend the seven sounds into each specific chakra and activate the seven keynotes. Your visualization will become more apparent, with more vibrant colors. The vision will be more realistic and attainable. Become accountable for your actions by bringing into existence what you visualize. The secret to the law of attraction is action and reaction to bring a thing into reality. When you activate the seven chakras, you open a new way to attract things and people into your life. The things and people are already there; they exist in real life, and you have not noticed them sitting or standing alone. When you activate the seven chakras, you activate the God within. You also release vital pressure points within the spinal cord, activating hormones and creating positive energy through color and sound. This positive energy creates your aura and manifests substance in your life. Whether health, happiness, success, or money, you may awaken your senses to accomplish your task.

The law of attraction can be attained when your vision is realistic and attainable. The more detailed the vision, the more likely it will be manifested. The patience to open your chakras for relaxation and visualization will take practice—the chakras and the spinal cord act as antennae to draw all that you have visualized. With patience, you can open the chakras and create a new energy field that opens you to a new level of higher nature. As you practice opening the chakras, a God-like nature brings you to a higher self of friendship with human nature, and human nature will assist you in manifesting. When you raise frequency, the law of attraction is in reach. The thing that you most desire already exists and will manifest itself. Transform yourself into information and personal reflection to create physical and material gain.

The law of attraction can be characterized as the divine attributes of free will thoughts creating that which exists within and without. The seven chakras represent the seven steps to the god within that manifests all things. It is the tree of life that eliminates faith, hope, charity, perfection, and renewal. Use chakra alignments to reach a higher state of clarity in your visualization process. When you can activate the chakras, it helps you clarify your reality within, exactly like the real world without. The purpose of using colors and sounds is to create a strong vibration for raising our frequencies. The goal is to enhance the natural and universal functioning of the human consciousness. The meditative practice of chakra alignment enhances the awareness of the five main senses and activates four additional senses: intuition, telepathy, clairvoyance, and precognition. With these additional abilities, you may use your intuitive knowledge that the universe offers in the real world.

The scientific method of laws of attraction, attracting, creating, and allowing, requires systematic observation, study, theories, and experiments that can be tested and reproduced. You will attract that which you think is the most important. Let your thoughts become repetitive and clear when visualizing. Remember that the human body is an energy center, and when you continuously focus on particular things, the vibration frequency is in tune with your thoughts. We attract that which we desire daily. We are not always aware of what we have attracted; therefore, when we activate the senses by practicing aligning our chakras and visualizing our desired results, they will appear, whether negative or positive. However, recognizing our empathy for others and treating others with utmost regard will naturally align us with the universal laws.

Universal Laws

Desire, seeing, hearing, smelling, tasting, and touching are considered natural laws, and these laws are not always an exact science. A person can be born without seeing, hearing, smelling, or tasting, for that matter, and never recover these natural senses. But universal laws are considered natural laws that constantly occur and recur. These universals are not seen, but they will always exist until the end of time.

"The heaven declares the glory of God, and the sky shows his handiwork."

(Psalm 19-1)

Listervelt Middleton stated that we should *"sharpen your eyes, tune your ear, so you will know what you see and understand what you hear."* Understanding the natural laws from a practical point of view will help you achieve your goals. You may be able to recognize these laws to your advantage for your benefit.

Twelve universal laws are natural and spiritual, and impact everyday life. You are summoning some of these laws when you practice meditation, visualization, affirmations, prayers, and hypnosis. When you begin to manifest, you want to understand that these laws may work on your behalf. When you pray for healing, success, wealth, and excellent health, you don't see it, but you know and understand that it exists for you. Confidence is more sustainable if you understand, acknowledge, and react to this law. When you are capable of recognizing natural occurrences of the universal laws, you may, for all purposes, manipulate these occurrences for your benefit. The law of attraction is only one aspect of the universal laws that allow you to have what is good for yourself and others. Therefore, consider yourself as part of the ever-evolving laws, and live under these laws.

The twelve universal laws are Divine Oneness, Vibration, Correspondence, Attraction, Inspired Actions, Perpetual Energy Transmutation, Cause and Effect, Compensation, Relativity, Polarity, Rhythm, and Gender. When you understand the first universal laws, the law of divine oneness, you realize that the universe is interconnected with every desire, spoken word, and belief, and impacts your every thought that creates your reality. Therefore, all universal laws are interconnected; for instance, the law of vibration lets us know that everything is in constant motion, vibrating at a specific frequency that creates our desires. Likewise, the law of correspondence directly relates to the fundamentals of oneness; the pattern is repeated throughout the universe as we constantly vibrate. Furthermore, we are using the law of vibration, and depending on the frequency, whether high or low, we are automatically attracting our existence. Independently, we are taking certain actions, and the law of inspired action brings into reality what we are working toward and putting effort into. This one specific law, the law of inspired action, requires constant meditation, visualization, and hypnosis before action. Moreover, when we recognize that we are creating through visualization what we desire, it comes from the inner person; it exists within, and the law of perpetual transmutation manifests the thing we desire from without. Finally, when practiced and activated, the first six universal laws set and create the backdrop for the remaining universal laws: cause and effect, compensation, relativity, polarity, rhythm, and gender. Be mindful that these universal laws are spiritual. According to these laws, consistent meditation is required, with visualization and hypnosis practiced through deep meditation and quantum jumping. For instance, in the physical universe, you may create steps to a program or a to-do list, whereas the spiritual universe requires meditation or visualization to gain wisdom.

> "When you break laws in the spiritual universe, you are injured somehow in the physical universe."

> ~Raymond Aaron

Activate More Brain Powers

> "There are no limits to what you can accomplish except the limits you place on your own thinking."

> ~Brian Tracey

You do not have to understand how the brain works by learning the physiology of the brain and its processes. You need only understand the processes of the human mind and the brain's functioning as it relates to the nervous system. Communicating, walking, or breathing may be difficult when the brain is not working correctly with the nervous system. The brain is the human-computer that connects and controls the center of the nervous system. The brain is not like any other organ of the body that can be transplanted back into the body. Once the brain is damaged, there is most likely a disability within the body.

Brain injuries, trauma, or damage to brain tissues can cause symptoms such as fatigue, stress, depression, and medical conditions such as weakness in the limbs or paralysis. We must look at the brain as the spiritual center of our existence. The hidden power holds the key to activating the god within. The brain functions because of the oxygen and blood supply it receives from the heart. The brain is a complex system of cells and nerves that constantly communicate with each other and other structures and systems of the body. Moreover, the brain and the nervous system make us function as humans.

When we breathe correctly, we provide the proper amount of oxygen to the brain to help it function properly. Our emotions, creativity, and actions are directly related to the function of the brain. When we activate the hidden power, we search for the god-like person we are to be. We activate the cortex of the brain. The cortex is the brain's outer layer, where we perceive speech, perception, long-term memory, and judgment.

We may activate the cortex by aligning the crown chakra by performing the deep breathing technique to inhale breath into the midbrain, visualizing the color bright red in this area, and exhaling while making the mantra sound aum-m-m-m-m. We focus on the outer cortex, but still activate the pineal gland. When we open this chakra, we activate the pineal gland and create a timing cycle that produces melatonin. This enhances light-sensitive melatonin, affecting sleep patterns and biorhythms and making our dreams more realistic. Although melatonin is of interest as a healing hormone, scientists speculate that the pineal gland, which produces melatonin, is also the control center that functions our physical, emotional, and mental selves. Finally, because the brain is so complex, as we understand more about the brain and its physiology, scientists know that the pineal gland, which produces melatonin, has much to do with the pituitary, thyroid, adrenal, and gonads.

Healing Power of Hypnosis

This is an exciting new concept to activate the hidden power within and manifest all that you desire. You will realize that it is within you to enjoy all that life has to offer you or all that you have dreamed of: excellent health, peace of mind, and enjoying life to its fullest. When we analyze and assess where we are right now, are we getting the best we ask, seek, and attract? (Matthew 7:7) Biblical text informs us to ask, seek, and attain access to what we ask. Pure determination alone will not help us obtain what we desire. When we activate the hidden power within with hypnosis, all things we ask for, see (visualize), or draw energy to will slowly manifest themselves.

Quantum mechanics describes the nature and functioning of the subconscious to the conscious mind by manipulating the subconscious through hypnosis, biofeedback, and transcendental meditation. The brain hemisphere synchronizes to create the distance between time and space dimensions. To heighten the state of altered consciousness, use hypnosis to assess the sensory-motor pleasure center of the cortex of the brain. To heighten our transcendental state of consciousness, we align our chakras. To heighten your self-confidence and cognitive power, activate your biofeedback through inner words. With practice and prolonged use of hypnosis, the results of your desired visualizations will manifest. Activate the hidden power of the God, Source, within you by meditating, visualizing, and now using this powerful hypnosis technique to create your new world.

When you use hypnosis, you realize that you are made in the image of your God, source energy. When life was breathed into you, you became the image of God, the god in you, who is all but not above all, and through all, and in all. (Ephesians 2:3) All you ever desire is in your subconscious mind, and to activate that which you desire, speak it into existence. Self-hypnosis is not yoga, but with repetition, we will tend to carry out and complete our task without stress and slowly activate actions toward our desired goals, unlike kundalini psychosis, where there are manifestations of illusory voices or auditory hallucinations. With self-hypnosis, you will start to work toward your goals. When using hypnosis, we must be careful to focus on one particular thing for it to manifest. Our vision must be clear and colorful to present the desired result. When we already affirm that it is so, then it must be. You are already healed because you have told yourself so. You recognize the number one reason for unwholesomeness; now let it be gone. You are already healed because you have told your brain how to recover your wholesomeness.

When you use hypnosis, you use your inner skills to program the subconscious mind to become active. The subconscious mind will receive a clear assessment of your visualization and provide the necessary knowledge to bring your vision into reality. You may be able to reach your highest probability using these simple techniques: complete deep breathing techniques, relaxing the body, and aligning the seven chakras during meditation while visualizing the area you want to heal; you will use a repetitive, hypnotic command to activate the brain to heal this area.

I will profess that I am not a hypnotist, but I have used hypnosis to heal myself from severe allergies, symptoms of post-traumatic stress disorder, and depression. When you begin to use hypnosis, refer to expert hypnosis or self-hypnosis books that are proven and safe. One of my favorite authors on hypnosis is Professor Tepperwein, an expert on the history of hypnosis and author of the book *Master Secrets of Hypnosis and Self-hypnosis*. I love that he gives many examples of how people have healed themselves and how some have used his book to gain wealth and prosperity. I have created some fantastic self-healing and self-improving recordings on my website that may help you get started.

If you are attending school, you want to enrich your personal life in the area of thinking. When you perform the exercise in the next section, ensure you are in a comfortable, quiet area without noise or interruption. Do not expect immediate results; watch for signs of results as you continue to perform the exercise. I am confident you will be thankful later. Refer this information to your friends and family, or visit my website for more perks and knowledge about hypnosis. It is not difficult for you to monitor the results of your progress; you want to write down any progress you have made toward the desired thing for which you have chosen to use self-hypnosis. You will want to use your session continuously for several weeks and keep a journal of your progression. As you continue to use your hypnosis at least once a week, preferably at night before bed, you will be surprised by the results, and you will want to make hypnosis a part of your lifestyle.

When you realize how special you are, that you are made in the image of God and the source God resides within you, you may use hypnosis to wake the God-person within and communicate with the God in you, fulfilling your every need. When using hypnosis, you communicate with the inner awakening of the Godchild, the God within, to perform what you desire. With the simple hypnosis technique, healing, joy, success, and prosperity can be yours. Like you, I was skeptical until I witnessed the results for myself. I was dying on the streets of Chicago after leaving the war in Vietnam, and then something special happened to me; I was awakened. I knew nothing about healing myself, but my hypnosis was for me to affirm that I was healing and recognize that when I have faith and do not doubt, good things will happen in my life. It was true; I am here today. You are special as well, and something special will happen to you when you practice the hypnosis exercises for your benefit. You will see the results, building confidence and reaching your goals just like I did.

We have all heard the story of how Jesus (Yahshua) walked on water during a storm to meet his disciples. One of his disciples doubted if it was Yahshua, and questioned his authority, and went as far as asking him to allow him to walk on water. "And Peter answered him and said, Lord, if it be thou, bid me come unto thee on the water. And he said, Come. And when Peter came out of the ship, he walked on the water to see Jesus. But when he saw the boisterous wind, he sank and cried, saying, Save me. And immediately Jesus stretched forth his hand, caught him, and said unto him, O thou of little faith, wherefore didst thou doubt." Matthew 14: 28-31

Hypnosis Exercise to Improve Your Intelligence and Aspiration

Only humans have the capability to change or alter their lives. All other animals live by instinct only. When you activate the hidden power of the God within, you increase and align your energy fields, elevate your frequencies, and create the life you want. By practicing hypnosis, you become the metaphysical you, ascending to a higher level of intelligence and inspiration. Using hypnosis, you communicate with God within, manifesting happiness, peace, joy, and harmony. You create positive thoughts of abundance, healing, and inspiration for the unknown to do your beck and call. When you hear the smooth, calm voice within, you create positive energy and enhance the body to a higher frequency level. The more you practice, the more benefit you will receive from a metaphysical, physiological, and spiritual perspective of your life.

You may be capable of ascending beyond the physical world and understanding the difference between the existence of things that are and things that are to be. You may experience that which you desire within and manifest it into reality. You may gain knowledge and intelligence in the metaphysical universe and use it to your benefit. You will do as it is from a physiological and human perspective. Though the mind is complex and sometimes confusing, you can use self-hypnosis to communicate with the inner self, heal, or gain knowledge. Often, when we think of hypnosis, we think of a person flashing a pendulum in a person's face and putting them to sleep. The person is given a command to respond to certain triggers. Once the trigger is activated, the person will respond to the command.

You will be using self-hypnosis in the same way as trained hypnosis; however, you will be your own moderator in your mind. You will be creating and giving your mind permission to give yourself intelligence, knowledge, and inspiration. Use complete breathing techniques to get into an alpha state of consciousness. Command your subconscious to search the cosmos for new knowledge and cosmos. As the metaphysical, you become more practical with consistency, the cosmos will give you the answers you ask for your success.

You may not be at your best; you may feel fatigued at times, feel burned out from work, or have some personal issues. We can use self-hypnosis to assist us with our energy and healing our bodies. We want our hypnosis session to focus on the physiological command of our organs, tissues, glands, and muscles to be at their best. In your hypnosis, concentrate on the part of the body that is most troublesome. Concentrate and command every cell in your body to be activated. Focus on the physiological aspect of hypnosis; be specific when you concentrate on the command for healing.

When you use hypnosis to search for answers for a project for the universe, or for healing and self-care, you are already in a state of spiritual awakening. You can recognize when the God within is giving you an answer. Once you know it is working for you and continue to practice, you have reached the spiritual you.   Then, you can heal your body physically and gain knowledge mentally. Your cells, organs, tissues, and glands will activate the spirit of God, who is one with you for all knowledge.

75

CHAPTER 8:
CREATING YOUR VALUE SYSTEM WITHIN

The Power of Gratitude

When using the context of gratitude, we are talking about the power of speech within ourselves. We are giving thanks to the god within. We are not just using the concept of words to create or manifest; we are communicating with the divine attribute of what is and is to come. When we give grace, we activate different brain parts to react to our spiritual and emotional being. When we say we are grateful for something, we link the forebrain, the midbrain, and the hindbrain. The hypothalamus is responsible for emotions and drive, hunger and thirst, body temperature, and self-balance. Actions are being performed when giving gratitude.

When we give grace to the unknown, the hidden power of God within activates the prefrontal cortex, giving high order to our cognitive functioning. The third eye is activated to create more abstract thinking, provide basic social behavior, and create more decision-making abilities. Our basal ganglia-motor functioning, movement, program selection, planning, and memory are retrieved. We should always be grateful each day for everything we have right now; it is important because it opens the temporal lobe through which the sincere sounds of humble spoken words, language, and emotions.

When you humble yourself every morning to your source energy, your creator, your Elohim, you acknowledge that there is a master of all things: the universe, the planets, the sun, the moon, the earth, and all that is in them. You are, in essence, grateful for a healthy body, a sound mind, and a forgiving heart.

You are verbally giving thanks for the small things in life and receiving more than enough money, more than enough food, more than enough fine clothing, and more than enough security to help others.

Give thanks to the new ideas, new opportunities, new identities, and new personal inventors of life. Be grateful for being alive and healthy; be grateful for this amazing day, every day. You are the master of your destiny and the maker of your new you. Be grateful that you can meditate, relax, and enjoy the happiness of life. You humble yourself to the abundance of the present, future, and always. Life is not a challenge; it's a joy, and I am thankful to be amongst the living, acknowledging my faults and defaults.

As you contemplate the many things that you are grateful for, always be mindful of doubt. Doubt is like a wall that can creep into the mind's crevices and slow down your blessings. Doubt, like fear, can kill your dream and destroy your faith. Doubt can create stress, depression, and uneasiness. To eliminate doubt, know that your creator, your source energy, and the hidden power within have been activated. You have already given thanks, and it is already settled.

The power of prayer

"The effectual fervent prayer of a righteous man availed much."

James 5:17

According to Wikipedia, prayer is an invocation (voice) or act that seeks to activate a relationship with an object or worship through deliberate communication, supplication, or command. In prayer, one communicates with a deity, spirit, or ancestor. Most often, one gives thanksgiving, praise, or admiration to their entity in a spiritual way. Prayer takes place in various forms, such as religious or personal rituals, and is performed alone or in groups. Prayer can involve a form of ritualizing acts or be performed in strict sequences. The scientific studies of prayer have mostly focused on the healing of sick and injured people. Most studies have resolved contradictory results.

When you show daily gratitude, it becomes the building block for the messages in the body; these include enhancing the hormones, enzymes, immune cells, and neurotransmitters in the brain. When we pray, it gives a vocal acknowledgment and assurance that we have a spiritual helper who is working on our behalf as a guide. When you dispense your admiration to an unknown deity, spirit, or your ancestors for supplication when others dismiss it, there is a union between self and the spiritual world that equates one with the body and mind of the divine. We create our sanctuary, a place of solidarity, peace, and a place of solemn where we can connect with the god within and allow it to guide us in reaching our desires. After presenting our prayer to the unknown, the ever-present, the almighty, and the most merciful, we are viscerally moved by our commitment to stay focused on the task at hand.

"Man's God in his divine parts," said Manley P. Hall. Man's soul is abiding within his own body. In the spirit world, man addresses his prayers. In his spirit, he is assured of the hope that is to come. Led by your motivation, aspiration, and faith, you become one with your spirit, achieve what you have prayed for, and gain immortality.

The Power of The Subconscious Mind and Affirmations

Anytime you give grace and humble yourself to your energy source, you control your subconscious mind. Your subconscious mind activates the power within when you persistently affirm what you desire. When the power within is activated, it assures you that you have the power to activate without; when you affirm that within the subconscious, you have a conversational language to take control of your reality when you have affirmed that what you say is true and that you are giving thanks for already accomplishing it.

Can you imagine a life of health, success, and abundance? Speak abundance by saying these words. "I have enough money to afford a beautiful home with a swimming pool, jacuzzi, pool house, and beautiful greenery surrounding my backyard. I have enough money to eat the best and finest of food. I have enough money to take my family on a long and joyful vacation, to shop for the finest of clothes, and still have money left over to save, invest, and help others. I am successful, prosperous, and happy."

I imagine myself healthy and vibrant. I can go to the gym three times a week, I am healthy, my heart is well, my muscles and bones are strong, and I do not have any disease, disorder, or syndrome. I am young, beautiful, healthy, successful, and strong. I give my mind permission to heal every cell in my body; I am energetic and can run for long periods. There is no soreness or pain in my body. I am in control of my subconscious mind to do my will, and it is so.

There is a natural motivation in all of us to develop the power to manifest our wants and desires. We constantly search for abilities that would help us influence universal laws. Affirmations are a great resource to provide self-interest in a subject and help us raise our vibration for action to obtain those desires. When you say you are grateful that source energy, God, or the god in you has given you wisdom, knowledge, and skills to help others. You will begin to believe this with your heart, mind, and soul. When you give positive affirmations to the subconscious, the subconscious identifies all errors or inconsistencies and acts. Therefore, your affirmation must be specific, consistent, and to the point. Confidentiality and privacy are irrelevant to the subconscious mind; it acts upon the positive and, most often, reacts to the negative. We control our subconscious mind by continuously inundating the mind with positive words. During relaxation, meditation, and visualization, continuously call into existence that which you desire through affirmations.

The Power Quotes for Success

"For verily I say unto you, that whosoever. Shall say unto this mountain, be thou removed and be thou cast unto the sea; and shall not doubt in his heart but shall believe that those things which he saith shall come to pass; he shall have whatsoever he saith."

Mark 11: 23-24.

Banish all negative thoughts and concepts from your mind forever and be happy.

"There are no limits to what you can accomplish except the limits you place on your thinking."

Brian Tracey

"Set your goals high, and don't stop until you get there."

Bo Jackson

"Now faith is the substance of things hoped for, the evidence of things not seen."

Hebrew 11:1

Your reality must be built in the inner mind and imagination to become you naturally. Be fascinated with what you want to do. Success, successful people, elegant people, see yourself in them: successful, sleek, and prosperous.

"Never ask yourself 'how', never deal with this word. Be still and see the salvation of the Lord; leave the show alone."

Rev. Ike, give a detailed description of the vision you want.

"Develop a passion for learning. If you do, you will never cease to grow."

Anthony J. D'angelo:

"The way of success is the way of continuous pursuit of knowledge."

Napoleon Hill,

'The starting point of all achievement is desire; keep this constantly in mind. Weak desires bring weak results, just as a small fire makes a small amount of heat."

Napoleon Hill.

"He who is wise in his own conceit, who approaches a subject with doubt and resistance, will learn little. There is not much help for him. But he takes up a subject with an open mind. Willing to learn anything that will contribute to his advancement, comfort, and happiness is wise."

John Alexander McDonald.

Be creative, creating the shape and form in specific detail of your reality once it appears and takes form in the mind. Use vigor and vivid, and detailed instructions to bring it to existence. Using specific quotes will ideally raise your frequencies to the level of motivation and manifestation.

Powerful Mindful Exercise for Intelligent

This is one of my program's most powerful relaxation, meditation, and hypnosis exercises, which you can learn about on my website. One of the first things my program teaches is for you to learn how to become an expert and successful advocate in any profession you choose. Being intelligent about certain subjects helps you communicate more effectively. Read this exercise several times, record the words on a recorder, and listen to the recording at least twice weekly. This exercise is guaranteed to boost your confidence and increase your intelligence.

Take a deep breath. Holding for the count of four, three, two, one; when exhaling, repeat the count of four, three, two, one. Take another deep breath, holding again for the count of four, three, two, one; again, exhaling for the count of four, three, two, one. Take another deep breath for the count of four, three, two, one; finally, while exhaling, count down four, three, two, one. Take a few seconds to notice any tension in the body. Now, while noticing your breathing returning to normal, begin to relax the body.

Close your eyes and notice the vibration throughout your body and the vibrations of your chakra areas. Relax the scalp of your head. Relax your forehead and let go. Relax your eyelids, and the tissues surrounding the eyelids let go. Relax your face, cheeks, chin, lips, and mouth; let go. Relax your throat area all the way to the back of the neck and let go. Relax your shoulders, arms, hands, and fingers, let go. Relax your chest, relax the inside of your chest, the organs, tissues, nerves, and cells in the chest area. Relax your abdomen, relax the inside of your organs, tissues, nerves, and cells, and let go. Relax the pelvic area and let go. Relax the upper, middle, and lower back, relax the spinal cord, and let go. Relax your thighs, feeling the vibrations in this area, and let go. Relax your knees and let go. Relax your calves; let go. Relax your feet, relax the toes of your feet, and relax your soles. Relax the heels of your feet. You are now totally relaxed; let go of all the tension in your body and relax.

The command of Self-Hypnosis

I am totally relaxed, resting, calm, and becoming increasingly relaxed; my eyes are closed. My body feels flexible; my arms and legs are flexible. I feel relaxed--nothing can distract me. I let myself be carried along in this deep state of relaxation. I am breathing slowly and regularly. I am quite relaxed--a wonderful, peacefulness of calm envelops my body.

In this state of peace and relaxation, I have an opening to my subconscious, which grows wider and wider as I continue. My words are settling into my subconscious and taking root there. My subconscious will carry out these commands and bring them into reality.

So far, I have been using only five or ten percent of the true power of my mind. Now, I will use more and more of my mind and all its power. I now have the high-power mind I have always dreamed of; I can think now with the best of the elites. I can now learn a huge new vocabulary; I no longer have to be ashamed of my mind, background, or memories. I can associate and communicate with the most elite scholars and be with the people most beneficial for my quest and success. I can encourage them to respect and listen to me and follow me. I have the mind I have always wanted, to give me the life I have always wanted.

Day by day, I study and write about the things I love most, affirming and acknowledging the spiritual scriptures that will enlighten and inspire others to have the best life has to offer them. This writing pleases me still more. I await each new day with new and great ideas that help others. I await each new idea with patience. I concentrate exclusively on what interests me most; nothing can distract me. Each of my words is definitely engraved in my subconscious. I will remember everything that I have learned and share it with others. I am slowly creating the life that is within me.

When I need to learn something or study, I will automatically block all other thoughts from my mind. My mind will be filled only with what I need to learn. Everything else will disappear for that moment from my mind. And after, I will think only about what it is that I have learned. I will open my mind to it and plant it like a great video camera for memory. I will automatically take all of it in and record it in my memory like a video camera records everything it sees and hears.

My mind will be devoted to taking it in, recording it in my memory, and calling it back to my full mind anytime I wish. All of my memories will be ready to spring into my mind whenever I need them. I can use all of them to write a bestselling self-help book that will help others solve their daily problems. I will continue to create new winning ideas. The necessary inspiration will come to me during sleep. I will resolve all my problems as a matter of course. Relax; I will be fully awake, aware, and energized at the count of three. One, two, three. Open your eyes.

The brain is the most potent access to activate the God in you. When you fully record this command, you will trigger the billions of nerve cells and neurons in the body. This exercise is most effective when you record it and listen to it every other day for twenty-one days.

CHAPTER 9:
ACTIVATE YOUR LEADERSHIP ABILITY

The Power of Knowledge

"My people are destroyed for the lack of knowledge: I will also reject thee because thou hast rejected knowledge. That thou shalt be no priest to me; seeing thou hast forgotten the law of thy God, I will also forget thy children."

(Hosea 4:6)

When we look at the definition of knowledge, it is facts, information, and skills acquired by a person through experience or education, from a theoretical or practical understanding of a subject through research. It isn't easy to acquire knowledge without research. When researching a subject of interest, use multiple sources of information about the subject and analyze whether the information is accurate. Once you have proven the information is true, you have acquired the knowledge you seek. Once you have concluded your research and found flaws to correct and expand, you have obtained the ultimate knowledge and opened the God within you.

To know is to have a vision, be what you want to be, have what you want, and desire what you most desire. See yourself out of poverty, see yourself healthy, see yourself happy, see yourself loving and being loved, and see yourself as a successful, prosperous person. See yourself with plenty of money; imagine you have plenty of money, nice cars, wear the best clothes, and go on exotic vacations. See yourself as you desire to be. You will continue to gain the knowledge to bring all your imagination to reality.

You should always be in search of knowledge, whether through reading, social media, or the news. However, always be mindful of whether the information you gather is valid, helpful, and marketable to others. This new knowledge may be a confidence booster for taking immediate action toward your vision and goals. Finally, structure this new knowledge to empower and promote your ideas.

Assessing Your Leadership Skills

Several visualization and self-hypnosis techniques may assist you in raising your vibration to a higher degree, in order to heighten your potential. Initially, the novice will have written a specific plan for their goals and used meditation, visualization, and affirmation to affirm their desires. There must be an acknowledgment that there is a higher power source than the self. But you may yet picture the person you want to be, the things you like doing, and the life you want. When you confirm in your mind and critically assess your attitude, character, and aptitude. You are designed to approach obstacles more aggressively.

Consistently visualize yourself having and doing the things you would like to do, have, and be. See yourself wearing the type of clothing you like to wear, and buy an item of clothing when possible. Every so often, visit the dealership that carries the type of car you want to drive. See yourself speaking to a large crowd, giving advice, recommendations, and knowledge of your accomplishments. Visualize the tone of voice you are using, feel the confidence continue to build, and notice how your attitude, character, and aptitude change as you practice your visualization.

Research has shown that what you constantly think about will manifest in your life, so be clear about what is on your mind and change it if it contradicts your desired goals. Shakti Gawain stated, "Every moment of your life is infinitely creative, and the universe is endlessly bountiful; just put forth a clear enough request, and everything your heart truly desires must come to you." Do you believe you have the skills, expertise, and knowledge to be the best you can be and help others? Do you think,

"If thou canst believe, all things are possible to him that believeth?"

(Mark 9-23)

Are you a dreamer without a dream? Are you always trying to think of new ways to make extra money and failing to create an ideal? Are you a procrastinator, multi-tasking a thousand ideas a minute, and never activating one? Are you a self-doubter, and do you not understand that you can manifest new skills and talent? Understand that you are, all in all, the creator of your destiny. The question is, do you have a vision comparable to the skill set that is helping you grow daily? If not, create a clear vision that is accessible, obtainable, and practical that you can use right now. Picture the person you want to be, visualize yourself as that person, and emulate that person every day until you become that person. Set clear and identifiable goals that agree with your dreams and aspirations. Write your goals down and visualize them daily. Napoleon Hill states, *"Goals are like road signs on a map pointing us in the way we should go."* Your goals should be broken down into management steps, short-term, intermediate, and long-term goals.

The quickest way to assess your leadership skills is to use self-hypnosis. Self-hypnosis is a continuous practice of positive thinking of an ideal you have set, in order to change your mindset. When you use self-hypnosis, you can remove all self-doubt, fears, and impractical negative thoughts. You can replace negative thoughts with positive ones to help you reach the quality of life you have visualized. You are creating your reality through self-hypnosis and enhancing your thought process toward pure action. Any skill you may desire is created through your mind, and self-hypnosis is a form of meditation with practice to help you develop the skills needed to accomplish your goals.

Creating Your Power Group

According to Google's definition, *"Mastermind groups are peer-to-peer gatherings of individuals who share common values and goals. They work together to obtain clarity, promote accountability, and take action to enhance moments in their lives and businesses."* When you create a mastermind group, the group becomes a haven for each individual to express their ideas and opinions without bias. Your group should be able to educate, improve skills, and give value to its members. The group can be created to invite experts to provide a sense of authority over the group's structure and purpose. It should be designed toward a specific goal and provide each member with a combination of educational and personal views.

Whether group members are extroverts or introverts, creating a powerful mastermind group requires accountability and actions. Some members may be extroverted and often speak openly and candidly about their ideas in a physical group setting. In addition, a physical group allows members to be open to personal and spiritual connections. On the other hand, some members of your group may be more introverted, and you may need to create a group that corresponds to virtual media. You can build and interact through Zoom and other internet sources to provide effective communication, goals, and actions. Physical accommodations like book clubs, yoga classes, or fitness membership are best for mastermind groups because you interact personally with members.

When we assemble ourselves together, we can encourage each other and provide a wealth of different points of view to give confidence and encouragement to each other. Having a mastermind group allows us to have consultation, knowledge, and recommendations we would otherwise have to pay a fee to attend. In a mastermind group, you can learn new ideas and trends that keep you up to date with lifestyle changes needed in your area of expertise. Practice creating a powerful mastermind group in your subconscious mind.

Take a personal inventory of the people in your mastermind group and seek information that will make you an expert in that field. Ask questions that are doable and may work in the real world.

First, use the deep breathing exercise to relax your inner being, align the chakras by breathing in the breath of life, its colors, and sounds, and then go into a deep hypnotic state. You can do this by recording and repeating the intelligent hypnosis exercises in chapter eight. Image in your subconscious mind the top-level experts in the field of your choice. These experts will make up your mastermind group. For instance, if you wanted to create a group of great speakers, you would choose the mastermind of Dr. Martin Luther King Jr., who wrote the I Have a Dream speech and delivered it in front of two hundred thousand people at the mall in Washington, D. C. What about Billy Graham, who for many years filled the arena all over American with his gospel speeches? If you want to create a group to help you become a millionaire, choose in your mind group participants that are already proven, such as billionaire Elon Musk, financier Warren Buffett, or the master mind of Mark Wahlberg. To make this an influential mastermind group in your mind, keep the participants to three or four. After you have practiced the intelligent hypnosis exercise several times, you may be able to hold your own, communicate effectively with these experts, and gain the needed education and information to act toward your goals.

Communicating Effectively

When speaking to a group member or any one person for consultation, advice, or recommendations, speak clearly. When you speak clearly, it is not just in the words you present in the details, specificity, and clarity; it is the inner standing relating to your messages. Considering the religious perspective of our entire existence, we realize it is built upon the word. When you practice the exercises in this text, you get a better inner standing of the God within, the awakening, and it gives you the words from a spiritual rim. You have to see yourself as an authority when delivering your presentation. When you consistently practice the breathing, meditation, visualization, and hypnosis exercises, words and deeds will awaken the inner person in you and give you a clear vision of the things you should ask to create your existence.

Words should be communicated at the highest value; if not presented properly, poor communication may negatively affect the person spoken to. Be clear about what you are seeking from this interaction. Look for words that will excite, educate, and promote positivity in conversations. Your communication should be clear, persuasive, and objective. Identifying popular itineraries based on your desired goals. You should go into the conversation determined to be an efficient listener and show functional responses. Although we value the way we present our presentation with words, being a great listener is also a valuable skill to have.

When you recognize what others say or do, particularly when you recognize their body kinetics, you are going into the conversation with an understanding of their purposes in the discussion. Not fully understanding the purpose of the conversation places you at a disadvantage. Certain basic mistakes may arise when conversing about work, school, or your personal life. You must surely understand how to bring value to the other person's purpose. In his e-book on writing, Raymond Aaron stated, "If you don't know exactly what you're trying to achieve with your writing, you probably won't achieve it." It is the same with spoken words. You likely won't achieve your purpose when you don't know exactly what you're trying to achieve in the conversation.

Stay in Control of Your Destiny

You have been meditating, visualizing, affirming, and using hypnosis for weeks, and nothing has happened. You have prayed and meditated daily on your vision board, but you are still not sure this is working. Remember, everything you have read and practiced so far is to activate the hidden power of the god in you. You are not to spend unproductive time worrying about what-ifs. You have activated the power of the inner self, the god within. You are to step out on faith and accept any opportunity without fear or apprehension.

When you set your goals, and they are clear and specific, you are most likely to succeed. Create a short-term goal that is doable within the project's first week. When you perform these chores, you have clarified what you want. Clarity is one of the four traits of successful people and should be updated throughout your project. The second trait of successful people is self-awareness; it is accomplished when you can recognize and implement opportunities and associations. Now that you can see tangible evidence of your work, your self-confidence builds, and you know that this short-term goal can manifest.

Building your authoritative self is important as you move into the next stage of your medium-term goal-setting,

Relax, relax, and do not let doubt and fear creep into your subconscious, you, the god within. Do not let misguided thoughts change your direction. The golden rule is to practice gratitude for what you have already accomplished. Gratitude is the conduit through which conversations are given to activate with the god within. No matter what is happening around you, be still and know that God has been awakened in you. (Psalm 46:10) When you feel excited and confident about your success, the process of attracting what you want begins to materialize. The subconscious, you, the god within you, is listening to your affirmations and prayers.

You must continue to hold your vision and imagination with clarity, focus, and control, always mindful of the law of attraction, orchestrating and unfolding all that you need to create your desires. You should always feel joy, honor, and happiness for others who prosper in your message of hope. You understand that you have value, and value is in you. When you believe you will make it happen, it will happen. Belief is a variable that is constantly repeated and re-enacted. You create subjective and objective views as your vision and imagination become a reality.

CHAPTER 10:
FOR THE LOVE OF MONEY

The Power of Money

When we look at the definition of money, every dictionary states that, formally, money is a current medium of exchange in the form of coins and banknotes. Informally, money can be any form of asset, property, or resource owned by someone or something. While money was once limited to coins and banknotes, its current usage refers to any currency, token, banknote, or the like that is accepted as a medium of exchange. Although we use money to accumulate what we desire, we are more likely to become wealthy if we focus on the informal definition of money. Try to make your vision from a thing perspective when performing relaxation, meditation, and visualization. What do you desire right now? When we focus more on what we expect, the money will surely come.

We can use money as an asset by investing in the market without worrying about it. We can also provide accurate mileage to our money by reflecting on its growth. Furthermore, we shouldn't rely too much on data from the changing market when we have lots of money. Making sound decisions when we have money is essential because money may become our myth. I once heard a wise man say, "You can make excuses, or you can make money, but you can't do both." Money is the last thing we consider when we visualize our dream life. We don't care where it comes from or how it landed in our bank account because we visualize things. We continue to focus on the things we most desire to be, do, and obtain. We must look at money as a spiritual journey in life; Dr. Richard Carlson, Ph. D., wrote the book *Don't Worry, Make Money: Spiritual and Practical Ways to Create Abundance and More in Your Life.* I think Carlson's book clearly shows the difference between abundance and wealth.

Money is an asset, and according to the definition, an asset is anything that has monetary value, such as any interest in real property or personal property that can be used to pay debts. We acknowledge that when Yahshua (Jesus) sent the disciples out to the world, he told them to *"heal the sick, cleanse the lepers, raise the dead, and cast out devils: freely ye have received, freely give. But provide neither gold, nor silver, nor brass in your purse. Nor scrip for your journey, neither two coats, neither shoes nor yet staves, for the workman is worthy of his meat."* (Matthew 10:8-10) When I read these words, it informed me that we do not need to worry about money in its material form. The 11 verses of Matthew say, *"And into whatsoever city or town ye shall enter, enquire who in it is worthy, and there abide till ye go thence."* Consequently, we would surmise that we should be worthy of our moral values to obtain what is value for our desires.

Live a Long and Prosperous Life

Everyone is hoping for a long and prosperous life before they leave this world for the outer world; the key is how we value our life and what it is worth to ourselves and others. When we can obtain the ten characteristics of a Godly attitude.

1) a peaceful mind

2) a caring heart

3) a spiritual revelation

4) a provider of substance

5) a desire to move forward

6) a desire to communicate with God

7) a sense of honesty and integrity

8) a person of honest intelligent

9) a person with a trustworthy   10) a love of self and others
   spirit

These attributes give us tools to use when communicating and interacting with others. We must align these attributes with our human nature and recognize the biological and environmental conditions, and our limited capacity to choose and create. When we focus on our internal determinants of behavior, such as a person's values, beliefs, attitudes, goals, interests, and individual perception of reality, we are most likely to be prosperous.

Your faith and belief in a source power, God, or an energy vessel more powerful than yourself give you substance. There will always be some traumatic experiences that come with life. However, your faith in a higher power can keep you strong. Your creator and the creation in you keep you strong and give you something to live for. Create a meaningful life with positive views of yourself and others. When we lose a sense of value, we lose a part of us. We must give ourselves credit, acknowledging God and the God in us, with power. Acknowledge that there is a greater power within you, with you, and throughout you. All your endeavors come through meditation, relaxation, visualization, and hypnosis, whether you perform them internally or externally, whether you recognize it or not.

We must learn to forgive ourselves and move on from any adversity.

"Forgiveness doesn't mean forgetting, nor does it mean hiding something that happened to us; forgiveness means letting go, moving on, and finding the positive."

Harold Bloomfield, MD

Surely, it will always get better for you; there will be more money, better health, and a sunny sky before long. We are made different in the eyes of God, in terms of the sources of energy we provide. Depression, generalized anxiety, panic disorder, suicidal and homicidal ideations, hostility, and psychotic disorders are all misdiagnoses; they are negative thoughts controlling the chemical substance in your brain and reflecting underlying dysfunctional beliefs and assumptions. These assumptions and beliefs are robbing you of your long and prosperous life. When beliefs and assumptions are triggered by situational events, a depressive pattern is put in motion that robs you of all your positive thoughts, reaches deep within the God in you, and activates the hidden power of self.

Using the complete deep breathing techniques and exercises in this book is important: relax, meditate, and visualize your dream world. Remember, *the only place success comes before work is in the dictionary; you have to fight to reach your dreams, and you have to sacrifice and work hard for it.* (Lionel Messi) Give an honest assessment of your accomplishments each week. Are you fearful, or are you confident? List your accomplishments, be productive, and prepare for mindful consideration. If your time is conflicted, change your cycle and prioritize important and pressing issues. Do the most important activities early in the morning hours and do fewer activities in the evening. Change how you greet your day; instead of good morning, say *Peace be unto you this day.* Strive to live a long and prosperous life; you can and will.

Morning Exercise

When you dedicate your life to growth, maturity, sustainability, and success, you must nourish your physical body with the right nutrients, minerals, and vitamins. In addition, when you prepare your mind for growth, maturity, sustainability, and success, you look toward meditation and prayer. The Shu, the breath of life, is the provider of sustenance to the physical body, as well as the brain. Fresh, sustainable air in the body triggers the ethers of the brain and nourishes a healthy mind. Meditating, visualizing, praying, affirming, or using hypnosis becomes easy for the novice when you are breathing correctly. When you breathe correctly before, during, and after meditation, you open the doors to spiritual enlightenment through aligning chakras, chants, mantras, tones, and earth sounds.

Although food is essential to nourishing the body for proper health, breathing is just as important. We need to breathe to live, so breath is also a physical part of our being. When you breathe correctly, aligning the chakras through chants, mantras, tones, and earth sounds, you are more likely to awaken the God within. The hidden power of the God within is accessible with proper breathing, and when you use the chants, mantras, tones, and earth sounds, your vibration frequency increases, and then you can call out to the Holy Spirit with grace. When you reach that divine state of consciousness, the superiority you develop and the ethical part of your understanding can be seen clearly by others.

Our ancestors noted that when a man gains knowledge through the observation of truth, his view of the world changes. Subduing the passion and leading the bodily energy upward so it would not be consumed by the lower nature, leading to a divine understanding of nature's forces. This exercise is simple and direct, but do not be fooled by its simplicity. This sun-rising exercise is embedded in the connection between the spiritual you and the God in you.

Find a comfortable position, either sitting or standing. Close your eyes and keep them closed throughout the exercise. Notice any tension or abnormal breathing. Place your arms and hands loosely to the side and relax. While inhaling, place your hand over your stomach, and as you inhale, feel your stomach slowly moving outward. Feel the breath of the Shu, coming through the nostrils and the diaphragm, pushing upward as the breath moves into the lungs; the shoulder is moving upward; once the shoulder moves to its highest point, hold the breath for four seconds, exhale until you have entirely released all carbon dioxide from the body. Repeat this process three times and sit still, observing your breath for several seconds.

Now repeat this affirmation: I am truly blessed; I am grateful to be well and healthy; I am successful, I am prosperity, I am happy; a large amount of money comes to me quickly and effortlessly every day, and when I use any of my money, it returns to me a hundredfold. I am young, I am beautiful, I am healthy, and I am prosperous. I am thankful the God in me has been activated. I will be faithful in my works and consistent in serving others, and in doing so, I may continue to have a healthy, successful, and prosperous life.

Be Still

Certain thoughts or feelings guide, protect, or bless you at any time of the day or night. When you are still, sitting in an altered state of mind and relaxed, and clear your mind, you are more likely to hear the voice of your source god. Pay attention to your thoughts and feelings; sudden thoughts may show you how to create opportunities for your success. You have to be still and trust in your instinct and institution. Powerful inner thoughts and voices are communicating with the God within, provoking and enticing you to be better than before. Do not be afraid to react when you hear the voice of God, ask for help, search out the meaning, and your answer will appear.

Be patient in everything you do, and with meditation, visualization, affirmations, hypnosis, prayer, and gratitude, opportunities will surely manifest. Take advantage of any opportunity that comes your way. When these opportunities appear, be thankful, and ask the creator and the god within to guide, protect, and lead you in the right direction. Notice any coincidence, be aware of the additional lost senses you have activated (telepathy, clairvoyance, precognition, institution), and use them wisely and to your advantage. Be true to yourself and understand that these are not just anomalies. Over stand that you have been summoned for this help. Be still.

Continue to pray daily in your own way, to your source, your God, and the God within, in silence, asking for guidance. Ask the God source, the God within, to speak to you, and be specific about what you want when asking for your desires. Ask for a clear mind for your decision-making ideas, and ask for warning signs when you are not sure it is the right decision for you. And ask for comfort in times of need, when things do not appear to go the way you planned. Seek in silence, and a better plan or opportunity will appear before you. When sitting in silence, ask and be open to new opportunities; when they appear, do not hesitate to step out and receive them. Create new ventures even if it is a difficult time for them. Read motivational books and the Bible, recognize the different verses that resonate with you, and act on them quickly.

Spend time alone in your imagination sanctuary, close your eyes, and take three deep breaths. Relax your body by releasing all tension. Concentrate on each thought that enters your mind; just let all thoughts float freely and effortlessly. Do not try to discard them; let them move out of the mind freely. Pay attention to thoughts that are not advantageous to your goals, but let them float. Those thoughts that resonate with your desires activate the feeling of joy within, and each time, focus on nothingness. Eventually, you will learn to sit in silence and recognize the true meaning of self. Be still, and let God. Just as the knowledge of geometry allows us to measure the distance between two points of a line, the knowledge of the principle of silence allows us to correspond and enable our inner self to reason intelligently from the known to the unknown.

Believe That You Have Already Received

The most intricate work is doing nothing; the worst-case scenario is that you are stuck where you are now and feel comfortable enough to stay where you are. Do you believe you are made in the image of God? The increased amount of information on the internet has affected us in various ways: our beliefs, behavior, and how we approach our daily lives. We tend to be stuck on what we view on social media, not knowing that we are continuously pounding our optic nerves and olfactory tract, which is conditioning the amygdala. Incidentally, the amygdala regulates the autonomic and endocrine functions, where decision-making is initiated, as the autonomic and endocrine functions for instinct and motivation. The information we take from the internet influences how we think about life and determines how we act daily. When we are taking in others' views of the world we live in, we are least likely to go out with friends and discuss new ideas of our own. We can now understand that we are what we always think about. That is why cutting back on internet and television time and subjecting yourself to meditation, visualization, and prayer are good ideas. We can create our own life just by meditating, visualizing, and using hypnosis. Before we can truly have a belief system that is dedicated to manifesting our dream life, we must first disconnect from the internet from our minds. We need solitude and peace of mind that can connect us to the divine within us.

To truly believe that we can have whatever we desire, we need a strong will to succeed and a spiritual and divine attribute that's easily replicated and repeated. One of the things we should do is make a practice of believing in a divine source that is in control of all things. The God in us, who creates wealth, our inner self, who is rich, the creator set to involuntary status. When the mindset is set to involuntary status, your mind is set on wealth creation with a wealth attitude. Change your mindset, know that you should have life, and have it more abundantly. When you think about wealth, not lack, and connect with true love, you attract more.

If you want large amounts of money, you have to love money like you love your body, your children, your spouse, or your parents. What you love and want is good for you, and the more you love it, the more you attract it. This is the god in you, attracting what is good for you, the spiritual in you. Focus on an abundance of money. If you want good health, you must love your body and believe you are healthy. Your body will desire healthy food, and you will begin to create a healthy lifestyle because you think about your body daily. You will begin to see a successful, wealthy, healthy body. Although life circumstances, bad judgment, and diminished access will continue to exist, your love for money, wealth, and happiness will become a strong positive asset in your life. Desire will overwhelm you. You are the master of your own destiny and the maker of your own life. Discard disturbing interpersonal relationships in your mind, and think about those that are good and lovable.

When you continuously think about what you desire, God will bring new associations into your life to assist you in having what you think about the most. You believe you have plenty of money, and God sends an associate to confirm and validate that the thing you desire exists for you, and opportunities for cash will appear. When something like this opens in your life, do your research, and when the information is truthful and valid, familiarize yourself with the new information and act; God will do the rest. You genuinely believe you have already received what you desire, which manifests with time and space.

Visualize It Constantly

Now we understand that the techniques of relaxation, meditation, alignment of the chakras, visualization, and hypnosis will enhance your ability to manifest. Your visualizations are more transparent and colorful, and your equilibrium is stable. When you create your vision board, make it as close to reality as possible, with all the personal details you want to manifest. For instance, if it is a car you are visualizing, go to your nearest dealer and get a brochure of that particular car. Frequently, we don't realize that to manifest our dream world, we have to activate the hidden power of God in us through persistence, meditation, visualization, affirmations, prayer, and hypnosis. The more persistent you become, the more you activate your autonomic nerves and endocrine nerve system to perform what you desire instinctively.

The human body is a capacitor, a resistor, and conductive of your thoughts. Every electron spiral has its frequency; you must learn to use the techniques in this book to raise your frequency. If you know the right frequency and can duplicate the frequency in an object in your visualization, the electron spiral resonates with the object until it becomes a substance. What you visualize within manifests itself without and becomes what you have visualized. When your idea is valid, the information is clear, the contents are coachable, and there is a network for distributing and marketing your vision, you will likely succeed.

It is best to visualize that you create your sanctuary and use it daily. Make the lighting soft and comfortable for your eyes and body, creating an atmosphere of solitude. If the sunlight is visible, imagine the rays proceeding from the sun to your inner self when aligning the chakras and the sounds in coherence with the colors. The more you align the chakras, using the complete deep breathing techniques, the clearer the visualization process, and the more detailed and colorful your dreams will become. Try visualizing the same dream you have created for yourself through your journaling process. Each time you visualize, add more details to your vision and continue to become aware of the hidden messages provided to you daily. You will begin to realize that your affirmations are truly becoming a reality, your prayers are beginning to be answered, and your visualization will become your reality.

The hidden power of the God within you has been activated and unlocked. You have become aware of the seven laws of the Kaybalion and the seven principles of the truth. The creator, the almighty Source, the God, and the God within you have given you the knowledge to transmute into the spirit of man. The actual principle that embodies the truth is that everything is in motion. When you visualize, you create your new world within and manifest it without. You understand the inner intelligence that enables you to reason with the inner self, the God in you.

ABOUT THE AUTHOR

Mac Drinker, BA, MS, has served as a veteran of the United States Army, worked as a therapist, and continued to help veterans and their families since 2006. Originally from Holly Grove, Arkansas, USA, Mac and his wife Donna reside in Marietta, Georgia. They have a family of eight children, four girls and four boys. Mac fell in love with relaxation therapy during his experience as a member of the Vietnam Peace Institute, North Chicago Veteran Hospital in 1985, and has been using meditation since, healing his mental and physical afflictions. As a result of his success with meditation, he has urged others to take advantage of meditation and relaxation for psychological and physical well-being.

Driven by his determination to succeed despite his post-traumatic stress disorder and doubt, Mac holds a bachelor's degree in criminal justice from Mercer University and a master's degree in community counseling from Argosy University School of Psychology. He is the author *of Invisible Wounds - History of Post-Traumatic Stress Disorder* and is an active travel advisor.

His new book, *How to Activate the Hidden Power of God in You,* can be found on Amazon or on Mac's website, activateyourhiddenpower.com. For workshops, consultation, or coaching, please get in touch with Mac at activatethehiddenpowerwithin@gmail.com.